Set Our Hearts
on Fire

Set Our Hearts on Fire

How to Kindle Revival in Your Church

RICHARD E. BIEBER

VINE
BOOKS
SERVANT PUBLICATIONS
ANN ARBOR, MICHIGAN

Vine Books is an imprint of Servant Publications especially designed to serve evangelical Christians.

All of the stories are true. Some of the names have been changed to protect the privacy of those involved.

Published by Servant Publications
P.O. Box 8617
Ann Arbor, Michigan 48107

98 99 00 01 10 9 8 7 6 5 4 3 2 1

Printed in the United States of America
ISBN 1-56955-075-1

LIBRARY OF CONGRESS CATALOGING-IN-PUBLICATION DATA

Bieber, Richard E.
Set our hearts on fire / Richard E. Bieber.
    p.   cm.
ISBN 1-56955-075-1 (alk. paper)
1. Revivals.   2. Evangelistic work.   3. Mission of the church.   I. Title.
BV3793.B46   1999
243—dc21   98-45619
                                                            CIP

Contents

PART ONE

Revive Me, Lord

ONE

Revival in Your Own Backyard

A s if an unearthly fire had dropped out of the sky, in 1904 a spiritual awakening exploded on Wales. It spread from town to town, taking hold of men and women and especially young people who had never given God a second thought. People would awaken in the middle of the night and start pacing the floor, crying out to God for forgiveness of their sins. Repentance began flowing down the roads of Wales like a river. Enemies were reconciled. Restitution was made for wrongs committed years before.

As the spiritual fire spread from town to town, churches could not contain the crowds that came to surrender their lives to Jesus. Worship often lasted far into the night as people laid their hearts bare before the glory of God and committed themselves to walking in his will.

The effects of this spiritual awakening spread across Europe, North America and even to India, stirring hearts to repentance and faith wherever it went.

For years some Christians had been praying for revival, but when it came, a twenty-six-year-old man named Evan Roberts seemed to be at the center of this awesome stirring of God's Spirit. An unlettered former coal miner, Roberts bore none of the marks of a modern celebrity evangelist. He did not know how to "work a crowd," and had he known, he would have repented at the thought. "Bend me, oh Lord!" was his constant prayer. His desire was that God's strength be made perfect in his weakness.

Roberts understood that this was God's revival, God's program. His responsibility was to fit into it. Jesus alone was directing the outpouring of divine fire on Wales and the world beyond.

God alone can measure the results of the Welsh Revival and the numberless outbursts of life from the Spirit before and since. But certain characteristics appear whenever the phenomenon we call revival occurs. I want to examine the essence of revival as it visits us as individuals and spreads through our churches.

On October 13, 1971, in a small Baptist church in Saskatoon, Canada, the Sutera twins, evangelists from Ohio, began what they expected to be a ten-day crusade. It seems that the fire that fell on Wales fell on this little church. A spirit of repentance swept through the assembly, as people crowded the altar confessing their sins, asking for forgiveness and renewing their commitment to the Lord Jesus. By the third night Ebenezer Baptist Church could not contain the numbers, and for the next seven weeks, the venue kept changing, as larger and larger facilities were needed to accommodate the swelling numbers. The "afterglow" of these meetings often lasted into the early hours of the morning, as people transacted business with the living God and became reconciled with each other. Wrongs were righted. Restitution was made wherever possible. These acts of obedience to the Spirit were followed by a joy which most of the participants in this revival had never known.

The revival spread south to Regina, Saskatchewan's capital city, east to Winnipeg, west to Vancouver and south into the United States. It crossed the Atlantic and ignited churches in Holland, always with similar results: cleansing and renewal in the church, fresh commitment and reconciliation in the lives of believers.

Revival—What It Is

Since the word *revival* is used in so many ways, let's begin with a definition of revival: what it is; what it does; and what it is not.

Revival is a work of the Holy Spirit in which hearts are urgently awakened to the reality of Jesus, moved to repentance and set free to live consistently in God's redemptive will.

Ideally this should happen whenever believers come together. Every worship gathering, every prayer meeting should be a mini revival. If we are gathered in his name and Jesus is in our midst, should not his Spirit awaken us afresh to his reality, move us to repentance and free us to live the gospel of the kingdom?

The Lord Jesus never ceases to do his part. But with the passing of time, followers of Jesus often relinquish their first love and settle into a "comfortable Christian walk" that is far beneath the call of the Master. He stands at the door and knocks and waits, while we pretend to be in full fellowship with him.

Revival occurs when we are awakened to recognize that our "fellowship with him" is an illusion; that the Master is still knocking at the door, waiting for us to open it. We repent. We open the door to the Master, meet him and love him anew and are empowered to follow him in doing the Father's will.

What Revival Does

Revival accomplishes three things:

1. It quickens our relationship with Jesus.

2. It brings us into unity with sisters and brothers in the body of Christ.

3. It moves us to reach out in love to those who have not yet met the Master and to those who have drifted away from him.

Again, these things should happen daily in the body of Christ. But our weak and ineffective outreach to the world is often a sign that something is lacking in our unity with each other. And the lack of unity in our life together as believers is always a sign that we need to cleanse and strengthen our relationship with Jesus.

What Revival Is Not

Revival is not the result of human engineering. We can pray for revival. We can prepare our hearts for a fresh encounter with the Spirit of God. But we cannot make it happen. Nor can we guide it, when it comes. It will come when God wants it to, where God wants it to, and it will take whatever shape God chooses that it should take.

Revival is not built around a human personality. Yielded human servants will always be found at the heart of a revival. But these servants remain useful to God's purpose only as long as they remain yielded and submissive to him. The minute they succumb to the temptation to control the revival, channel it where they wish it to go or put their personal stamp upon it, the revival will begin to diminish.

A revival cannot be preserved by human by-laws and constitutions. We can make all the rules we want to in an effort to insure that the revival remains doctrinally sound and spiritually alive. But the sustaining power comes from above and remains among us only as long as we are obedient to the living Word.

Thirst for Revival

In our rapidly changing world there is a growing thirst for something with more depth and integrity than what is commonly equated with churchgoing and respectability.

The phenomenal growth of Promise Keepers from a handful of men in 1990 to millions less than a decade later is one sign among many of the yearning for life from God and the power to live the life to which Jesus calls us. Bill McCartney, the ex-football coach who founded the movement, says he seeks to "present to the Lord godly men on their knees in humility, then on their feet in unity, reconciled and poised for revival and spiritual awakening."

Many of us hear about revival taking place in a certain city or a certain church, and we wish we were there. We wish we could experience what we read about in reports coming in from Africa and Russia and Brazil. Surely God can see that we need revival as desperately as those "favored ones" who are already igniting with heaven's fire.

How long can a person survive where the spiritual diet is poor? If week after week, we go looking for living bread and come home hungry, will we not soon waste away spiritually? "I need to be fed," is the complaint of a host of believers who fold up their tents and move on every few years in search of better spiritual food.

More life. Clearer vision. Where can I find it?

Without a doubt, there is a revival "out there." It is breaking out in many places, flowing together, gathering momentum. One day soon we may all be part of it.

But there is also a revival close at hand. From Scripture, and from the Spirit's witness in our own hearts, we learn that the revival close at hand requires our full attention. If we focus on the revival "here," we will soon be part of the revival "out there," even if we never leave our hometown. "If you then, who are evil, know how to give good gifts to your children, how much more will the heavenly Father give the Holy Spirit to those who ask him!" (Lk 11:13).

The search begins, not in some other place, but exactly where we are. Revival is closer to us than we think. As Jesus builds up to his promise that the heavenly Father will give the Holy Spirit to those who ask him, he tells us that no one is left out. "For everyone who asks receives, and he who seeks finds, and to him who knocks it will be opened" (Lk 11:10). But Jesus also encourages us to be persistent, like the man pestering his friend at midnight for bread to feed an unexpected visitor. Keep at it. Don't quit.

I remember a man who took that exhortation very seriously. Aubrey had been attending the Church of Our Saviour for only a few weeks, but it was clear that his heart had been crying out for a long, long time. He wasn't sure what he was looking for when he came to the study for a talk, but he knew that, whatever it was, it would have to come from God.

The following Sunday Aubrey went forward and knelt at the front of the church. This was nothing new. He had done this before; he was knocking, he was seeking. But this time something happened. He began to tremble, and while voices around him were singing and praying, Aubrey heard a voice from somewhere within which said, "You're looking for my grace, and I give it to you now."

On his return home, his wife knew immediately that something was different about him. Here was the same face, but her husband's heart seemed softer. "Aubrey, are you all right?" she asked.

Aubrey smiled. "Believe me, I've never been better."

The test came in the days that followed. If what came to Aubrey that day, as he knelt and trembled, was truly the presence of Jesus, then the life of Jesus would begin to manifest itself in Aubrey's daily walk. Eileen would experience a kinder, more thoughtful husband. Fellow employees at the bank would see a man beginning to change. Aubrey would hear Jesus speaking to him through the Scriptures. Prayer would become his mainstay.

I can remember, as I watched this happening to Aubrey, that it wasn't all peaches and cream. He had his struggles. But there was no doubt in my mind that this man traveled a new road as one who had found renewal through an outpouring of God's Spirit on his life. All of us who knew him could see Aubrey's life beginning to manifest the love of Jesus on a daily, down-to-earth basis, in his home, at church, at the bank, among his friends. And his fire ignited our hearts as well.

Lighting the Flame of Revival

Who isn't thirsting for more of this fire? Even the most joyful charismatics yearn to find, beyond their moments of ecstasy, a daily life that burns with a steady flame, a flame that imparts a clear awareness of God's call on their lives and his power in their hearts, so that they can get something done for his kingdom and persevere through the coming storms. Lord, set our hearts aflame! Cause the Shekinah glory to descend and ignite us with unquenchable fire!

The answer to this common heart-cry is rapidly manifesting itself across the earth. The fire is falling with unprecedented power in unexpected places and upon people who might seem to be unlikely candidates. People like you.

God wants to use you to bring fresh life to his church and signs of healing to the multitudes beyond it. He will accomplish through you far more than you would dare to imagine. All you have to do is fit into the program—God's program—which is astonishingly different from all the humanly initiated "programs" for revival.

God's program is clearly revealed in Jesus and the way he went about things. In this book I want to focus on God's program for revival as revealed in Jesus and as it applies to our lives today. Put in simplest terms, the Son emptied himself of his glory, became one of us, received the fire and spread it. He never promoted himself. He used no gimmicks. He never took his cue from his audience, never tailored his approach to their whims. He looked only to the Father for every word he spoke and every deed he performed. And he did all this as the Son of Man, even though he was indeed the Son of God.

Jesus walked by faith, even as we need to walk by faith. Jesus, as the Son of Man, depended entirely on the direction and power of the Holy Spirit, even as we need to depend entirely on the Holy Spirit. His obedience took him to a cross, but it paid off in resurrection life—not only for him but for us, his disciples. This resurrection life is the revival we're after, the fire from heaven we need. And it's ours in abundance, provided we are willing to do things his way, instead of our own.

His way is both glorious and costly. Glorious because it floods us and surrounds us with the blazing fire of heaven—joy in God's Holy Spirit—every hour of the day and night; costly because it lays on each of us a cross, a death, which we carry around in our hearts as long as we remain in these bodies of flesh and blood. Our lives are no longer our own. They belong to him. Literally. In a mystery that confounds the devil himself, we are crucified with Christ; it is no longer we who live, but Christ who lives in us. And the life that we now live in these bodies of flesh and blood, we live by faith in the Son of God, who loved us and gave himself for us (see Gal 2:20). We begin to have the fire. Revival burns within us.

In this book I want to show how revival from God is poised and waiting to ignite our personal lives the moment we are willing to yield to it. We may be removed from the "hot spots" of revival by time or distance. But each of us is in a place where it can happen. I want to go on to show how every genuine revival in the individual leads to cleansing and increased life in the body of Christ. The Lord Jesus will set your heart on fire so that you can be a torch in his hand. His desire is to cause the revival to spread to others through you in simple, undramatic, practical ways.

As an example of how revival in a solitary life begins to spread through the entire body, consider Lily. When I first met Lily, she struck me as a prim, precise closed book. She was a private person. She had learned through costly experience what can happen when you open your heart to the wrong person. She was competent on her job, got along well with everybody in the office, but no one really knew what was going on behind those piercing eyes and that quick smile.

Through a singles group, Lily found her way into a small Bible study that met on Thursday evenings around a table in the basement of a church she never attended. For weeks Lily hardly said a word. But when she spoke, it was evident that this private person was on a serious search.

Then it happened. How it happened, Lily herself would be hard put to explain. But one evening she opened her mouth and began talking about the needs around her and about her own thirst. The curtain behind the eyes opened, the smile became warm, as Jesus began to manifest his love to her—and through her. Before long, anyone could see that private Lily was becoming a one-woman welcoming committee for the kingdom of God. She began reaching out in love to her sisters and brothers in the group, to her neighbors, to friends from work. The flame in Lily's heart was contagious. Almost without effort she brought encouragement and hope to people around her.

You may protest and say that Lily's quiet transformation is hardly a Welsh Revival. True, but if the Spirit that raised Lily from spiritual death is the same Spirit of Jesus that created the Welsh Revival, who knows the victories that may yet be won by this woman? And who can measure the life which even now flows from heaven through her obedience into others in need?

We may well be approaching a time of revival of which the Welsh Revival was but a minute foretaste. Reports are coming in of hundreds of new congregations springing up in Russia in the midst of grinding poverty and renewed harassment from the state. In a single year new believers on the continent of Africa are numbered in the hundreds of thousands. Decades of oppression have only served to strengthen the house church movement in China.

As we hear of these and other grassroots movements among believers, we have reason to hope that a widespread spiritual awakening has already begun. But the revival that requires your full attention is the revival that God desires to bring to you, the spiritual awakening that is prepared to visit your own backyard, your kitchen, your church. That's the revival on which to concentrate. Because, in very fact, that revival is already closer to you than your own breath. It is prepared to manifest itself to you and ignite your heart with the same fire that consumed Elijah's sacrifice and fell on our brothers and sisters at Pentecost.

Are you ready to receive it? Are you willing to let it spread through you?

TWO

God Has Something Better for You

My friend Al and I were out making calls on a Friday afternoon. We knocked on a door, and as we stood there waiting for it to open, a shiny Thunderbird pulled up to the curb.

"They're not home," said the driver, and then he added, "Whom do you represent?"

"Jesus," we answered.

He didn't laugh, nor did he drive off in disgust. He sat there stunned for a moment.

"Yeah? Tell me more."

It turned out that Arnold had once been a pastor and evangelist. But for the last thirty years he had refused to attend any church. His wife and two children were active believers, but Arnold had long since been defeated by the gap between expectation and reality.

Like most of us, Arnold yearned to experience God. In thirty years of isolation he had not lost his thirst, but he wanted more than talk. He was tired of hearing about God's wonderful promises. He wanted to see them made reality in his life and in the lives of others. Arnold was impatient with professing Christians who, in his view, had settled into a rut of mediocrity. He would rather stay away from church than go on torturing himself with those promises of life and power, while in fact his soul was dry and empty.

Arnold has a lot of company. We may still be going to church, praying, reading our Bibles and attempting to show compassion toward the people around us. But like Arnold, many of us are conscious of a gap between the high promises of God and what we are actually experiencing in our daily lives.

Here's what many of us are experiencing:

We struggle with unbelief. We're like the preacher who expounds for twenty minutes on "Seek ye first the kingdom of God, and his righteousness; and all these things shall be added unto you" (Mt 6:33, KJV) and spends the next half hour pitching for money. Our daily decisions betray a lack of trust in the simplest promises of God. "Look at the birds of the air: they neither sow nor reap nor gather into barns, and yet your heavenly Father feeds them. Are you not of more value than they?" (Mt 6:26). God promises to provide for us so that we can be relieved of our anxieties about tomorrow and pay attention to the call of the kingdom. But instead of leaving tomorrow in God's hands and going about the business of the day with childlike trust, we worry and fret over things that are beyond our control.

We have little or no awareness of God's love. Jesus teaches us to pray "Our Father who art in heaven." He promises that our heavenly Father watches over every sparrow, knows the number of hairs on our head. Yet our awareness of that fatherly love is often weak. Hidden beneath our professions of faith are the questions: Does he really care about me? Does he understand what I'm going through? We know that the Spirit of the Son in our hearts should be crying, "Abba! Father!" (Gal 4:6), but for long seasons in our lives we feel like orphans.

We are afraid. The first time I met Carlos he was carrying a hefty stick. He came into the room, sat in a chair, laid his stick on the floor and started to talk. When the conversation was over, Carlos picked up his stick, shook hands and marched out the door, swinging a stick that had pounded every block of West Vernor Highway and knew every path running through Clark Park.

Carlos and his stick were inseparable. Somebody might be following him. An enemy might be waiting in the alley. One has to be prepared.

The stick we carry might be invisible, but it's there. Something inside us is tense and on the alert for the big disappointment, the sudden shock. If things are going badly, we wonder what's going to happen next. If they are going well, we're already bracing ourselves for the end of the winning streak. We carry our invisible stick for fear that tomorrow will not be safe. Inwardly we keep looking over our shoulders, because we know danger stalks us.

Our hearts are distracted. There are bills to be paid, TV programs to watch, furniture to buy, repairs to be made on the car. We know we should be able to take care of the business of life and still be focused on the kingdom. After all, Paul made tents for a living. Philip had a wife and four daughters. Lydia had a business to look after. They stayed centered on Jesus. Yet the distractions of life consume us, and God fades into the background.

Jesus warned us about these thorns which will choke the growth of the good seed. The "cares and riches and pleasures of life" (Lk 8:14) he called them. He rebuked Martha for being "anxious and troubled about many things" (Lk 10:41) when only one thing is needful. But we find it almost impossible to follow Mary's example and sit still, listening to what Jesus has to tell us—about our lives, about our future, about what he is willing to do for us, so that we can live a life that's centered on him. How can we walk the walk of faith when we're so distracted?

Our resolve to obey is weak. Jesus tells us that the spirit is willing but the flesh is weak. And yet, our spirits cannot make progress in the things of God unless the flesh comes along. Resolve means that I bring my body, mind and spirit together in an act of obedience. I decide to do this thing, and I do it. I *will* seek God's face. I *will* forgive my brother. I *will* speak the truth consistently, without embellishment or exaggeration. I *will* abandon the unclean thought. What a disappointment to discover that my resolve is not nearly as strong as I thought it was. "For the good that I would I do not: but the evil which I would not, that I do" (Rom 7:19, KJV) Many of us are trapped in a weakness of resolve that makes a mockery of our good intentions.

We are haunted by our ineffectiveness. "By this my Father is glorified, that you bear much fruit, and so prove to be my disciples" (Jn 15:8). Have we made a difference in anyone's life? Have we even imparted to our own children the rich treasures of the kingdom? We know that to follow Jesus involves more than getting saved and staying spiritually "sanitary." We need to bear fruit for the kingdom of God. What's missing? Why isn't this happening?

Why is our experience so far beneath God's call and God's promises? Has God forgotten us? By no means! Our heavenly Father is ready to lift us into something far better than this desert of mediocrity. If we cooperate with him and do things his way, he will quickly bring us to a place where the promises of Jesus are fulfilled in our daily lives.

In the following chapters I want to describe how God will do this. But first let's consider what this new life God gives us looks like. And remember, this new life is not something far off. It is near. It comes with the revival which has your name on it and can be your experience before you finish this book.

You Can Hear the Master's Voice

"My sheep hear my voice, and I know them, and they follow me; and I give them eternal life, and they shall never perish, and no one shall snatch them out of my hand" (Jn 10:27-28). Be certain of this, you can hear Jesus speak to you. It may not be an audible voice or a vision, but you can know that the Lord is near and giving you clear direction for your life. He may speak through a word of Scripture or circumstances. He may guide you through a friend, or a sense of peace or restlessness in your heart. No means is beyond God. Sometimes he warns us; other times he encourages us in love or directs our attention to a need. As we learn to listen carefully for his voice in every arena of our lives, we can learn to hear it and heed it.

In the old covenant only certain men and women were

"seers" who had special relationships with God. It was their job to receive a word from God and pass it on to the people. But in the new covenant every follower of Jesus is given an ear to hear the Master's voice and wisdom to discern between that voice and every other.

You Can Experience Christ's Love

"I will not leave you desolate; I will come to you" (Jn 14:18).

One time I picked up the phone and called a man whose wife and child had been killed in an accident. I had never met this man, but I felt somehow that I was to contact him and try to offer my condolences.

At the end of the conversation he said, "You really love Jesus, don't you?"

Of course, I answered, "Yes."

But after I had hung up, I scratched my head and asked myself, Was that an honest answer? Do I love Jesus the way this man seems to think I do? Do I really have a sense of Jesus' love for me? That phone conversation was like a prod from the Spirit of God.

It was unlikely I would ever love Jesus the way that man seemed to think I did until I had a clearer awareness of Jesus' love for me.

"We love, because he first loved us" (1 Jn 4:19). But to know that "love of Christ which surpasses knowledge" (Eph 3:19)! How?

I began to realize that it comes as you thirst for it. When I discovered that the love of Christ was still a distant thing for me, that I needed desperately to know that love, the Spirit soon answered the cry of my heart. "I will not leave you desolate; I will come to you" is a promise Jesus gives to every one of us—a promise he keeps.

Through the Spirit Jesus expresses his love for you, a love that made him die for you, a love that longs to heal, restore and refresh you as you open your heart to it.

For this reason I bow my knees before the Father, from whom every family in heaven and earth is named, that according to the riches of his glory he may grant you to be strengthened with might through his Spirit in the inner man, and that Christ may dwell in your hearts through faith; that you, being rooted and grounded in love, may have power to comprehend with all the saints what is the breadth and length and height and depth, and to know the love of Christ which surpasses knowledge.

EPHESIANS 3:14-19

Paul prayed that the Ephesians would experience that freshness of the Spirit for which we thirst. It's there for the asking, when our hearts yearn for him.

You Can Walk in Christ's Peace

"Peace I leave with you; my peace I give to you; not as the world gives do I give to you. Let not your hearts be troubled, neither let them be afraid" (Jn 14:27).

When the risen Jesus stood among his disciples and said,

"Peace be with you" (Jn 20:21), this was not just a greeting. Jesus was giving them a gift. Peace. His peace had the power to calm a raging storm on Galilee. And it has the power to restore our hearts.

We have all met Christians who have this peace. They walk into a room where people are shouting accusations at each other, and the atmosphere begins to change. Mom comes home with a smile on her face, and the children forget why they were fighting. Her peace stills troubled waters. And when that peace is the peace of God, she brings some of heaven into her home.

You can have a supernatural calm in every situation. Things may be falling apart in your circumstances. Maybe your boss is blaming you for his own mistakes. Or the stock market has taken a dive and the whole world is in a state of shock. Or another round of "downsizing" is about to begin. Or your best friend has taken offense at something you said at lunch last week. Yet deep within you still have peace, because this peace does not depend on anything that happens in this world. It comes from the Lord of Lords. And it holds you in its comforting grip, keeping you calm though the storms rage around you.

You Can Serve the Lord

"Truly, truly, I say to you, he who believes in me will also do the works that I do; and greater works than these will he do, because I go to the Father" (Jn 14:12).

Jesus told the disciples to stay in Jerusalem until they were "clothed with power from on high" (Lk 24:49). How could they possibly preach the gospel, heal the sick, cast out demons and make disciples of all nations without the power of the Spirit of God? They waited in Jerusalem, the power came and they went out and got the job done. What God gave to them, he will also give to you. You can be clothed in power from on high so that you can accomplish everything Jesus sends you to do.

You will not need to seek out opportunities to employ this power from on high. They will come to you in the form of people with wounded souls and troubled hearts and broken bodies. You will have the joy of seeing the life of heaven flow through you to others around you. By this power you will bring good news to the poor, deliverance to the captives, sight to the blind, freedom for the oppressed and hope to the downcast. In your revived life the gap between expectation and reality will begin to close.

Believe that God has something far better than the desert of mediocrity in which so many of us have been wandering. Believe that the time has come for the promises of Jesus to be fully realized in your daily life.

THREE

Preparing the Way

They said to him then, "Who are you? Let us have an answer for those who sent us. What do you say about yourself?" He said, "I am the voice of one crying in the wilderness, 'Make straight the way of the Lord,' as the prophet Isaiah said."

JOHN 1:22-23

In chapter one I defined revival as the work of the Holy Spirit in which hearts are urgently awakened to the reality of Jesus, moved to repentance and set free to live consistently in God's redemptive will.

Why isn't this happening all the time in each of our lives, in all of our churches? After all, isn't this God's desire? Did he not send his Son into the world to suffer and die and rise again to open the door for us to exactly this experience? Why isn't the Spirit continuously revealing Jesus' nearness to our hearts, moving us to repentance, setting us free to walk consistently in the Father's will?

God continually sends his Spirit to us, to revive us. He desires (more than we could ever know) to flood us with his life. But if our hearts are cluttered with self-centeredness and self-righteousness, the Spirit has no access. If we are unaware of the amount of this world's debris which lies within our souls, it becomes even more difficult for the Spirit of God to convince us of the steps we need to take to prepare the way.

Before our Lord Jesus could begin his ministry, John the Baptist was sent to call the people of Israel to prepare their hearts for his coming by repenting. And every revival since has been preceded by people preparing the way, men and women at prayer. Sometimes these people are visible. Sometimes they are seen only by God.

It was no accident, for instance, that the Canadian revival of the early 1970s made its first appearance in the small Ebenezer Baptist Church in Saskatoon. This church was pastored by a man who saw the need for revival and understood the things that hindered its coming.

Five years before the revival broke out, Pastor Bill McLeod and his people were on their knees crying out for fresh life from God. Faithfully and consistently these men and women prayed, privately and together in a weekly prayer meeting, that new life would fall upon the people of God. All the repenting and reconciliation that was to take place when the revival arrived was already occurring in the hearts of these intercessors. They were preparing the way because they saw the need and were aware of the obstacles to spiritual health that existed in the professing church—and in their own hearts.

Before we can experience personal revival, a similar preparation must take place in our hearts. Our prayers for personal renewal need to be accompanied by specific changes in specific areas of our lives. Here are some examples.

"God, I Thank Thee That I Am Not Like Other People!"

A major obstacle to personal revival is our secret belief that, compared with most people, our lives are not so bad. If God is measuring us against the rest of the world on a scale of 1 to 10, we come out somewhere between 7 and 10. We might be hesitant to admit it publicly, but we're fairly confident that we deserve blessings and good treatment from God. After all, we sometimes go out of our way to help needy folks. We support the church. We know our way around in the Bible. We pray. People even look to us for guidance. Doesn't this modest goodness count for something?

> Two men went up into the temple to pray, one a Pharisee and the other a tax collector. The Pharisee stood and prayed thus with himself, "God, I thank thee that I am not like other men, extortioners, unjust, adulterers, or even like this tax collector. I fast twice a week, I give tithes of all that I get." But the tax collector, standing far off, would not even lift up his eyes to heaven, but beat his breast, saying, "God, be merciful to me a sinner!" I tell you, this man went down to his house justified rather than the other.
>
> LUKE 18:10-14

As long as I think my righteous deeds give me a claim on God, I hinder the flow of God's grace into my life. My only claim on God is the cross of Jesus. Jesus died on that cross for me, because his atoning death was my only hope. Jesus died on that cross to deliver me from my preoccupation with myself, which is the root of all sin. And my sin is most blatant when I congratulate myself in God's presence (as the Pharisee did) that I am morally and spiritually better than others around me.

I am a sinner saved by grace. Any righteous deeds I perform are made possible only by that grace. Apart from that grace I can do no good thing. I serve God out of thanksgiving as one who is absolutely indebted to that grace. If I lived on this earth a million years in self-giving service, I could never pay back the debt I owe to my Lord Jesus for his death on the cross for me.

Personal revival can never come to us until we begin to see that all our "righteousness" evaporates in the presence of a holy God. "For thus says the high and lofty One who inhabits eternity, whose name is Holy: 'I dwell in the high and holy place, and also with him who is of a contrite and humble spirit, to revive the spirit of the humble, and to revive the heart of the contrite'" (Is 57:15).

Your Program or God's Program?

If we are serious about experiencing personal revival, we have to decide whether we are willing to allow God's program to take priority over our own. For in many of our lives our own program always manages to come out on top. I'll serve you, Lord, but you need to know that Wednesday night is my bowling night. Or, Here's how I plan to serve you, Lord. I plan to help make New Life Christian Assembly the largest church in the city. Or, I'll serve you, Lord, but you might as well know that I work with adults, not with children.

Imagine a genuine servant outlining to his master the parameters of his service!

One time the phone rang, and the man on the other end explained that he had visited our church several times and had decided that he would like to make our church his home. He also informed me that he was skilled in the area of finance and offered to be our treasurer. I thanked him for his kind offer and explained that our church already had a treasurer who was faithful and competent. We'd be delighted to have him just come and be among us.

No, he insisted, if we couldn't use him as treasurer, our church was probably not the place for him.

He was right.

God's program and our program are not only different, they are incompatible. If God's program is to take hold of our lives and change them, our program has to go. Repentance is more than turning away from obvious sins. It is turning away from everything in my life that has me in the center of it, so that God can be in the center. I need to repent of my insistence on doing things my way, seeing things from my point of view, trying to make the kingdom adjust to my habits and preferences.

By your grace, Lord, I'll do it your way, see things from your point of view, adjust my habits to your plan. Your will, Lord, not mine—in all things!

Radical Commitment to Jesus

Two kinds of people followed Jesus on his journeys through Israel: groupies and disciples. Groupies loved to watch and listen and "hang around." But whenever Jesus' words became too demanding, or whenever persecution appeared to be imminent, the groupies disappeared (see Jn 6:66). Disciples were the people who were committed to Jesus—radically committed.

Jesus does not send his Spirit to Christian groupies, only to radically committed disciples. "He who loves father or mother more than me is not worthy of me; and he who loves son or daughter more than me is not worthy of me; and he who does not take his cross and follow me is not worthy of me. He who finds his life will lose it, and he who loses his life for my sake will find it" (Mt 10:37-39). That is, commit your life to me and withdraw from every attachment that tries to compete with your commitment to me. Leave your old life behind.

My friend Bernie is not much of a talker, but when he opens his mouth he usually says something worth hearing. Men often go to Bernie's barbershop not just to get their hair cut, but to pick his brain about the things of God. They know Bernie won't sicken them with platitudes.

Perhaps they find Bernie easy to talk to because there was a time when he was on the outside looking in. For years Bernie went through the motions of churchgoing simply to keep his wife happy. He didn't claim to be a Christian. It's just that things went better with Sonya and the kids if he went along on Sunday morning. So he'd sit there half asleep. He'd stand for the hymns and try to stay awake for the sermon. But one thing Bernie refused to do: he would not take communion. To him, taking communion meant that he really "believed this stuff." And he didn't.

Bernie knew Sonya was praying for him. Fine, let her pray. If it hits me, it hits me.

One day, to his own amazement, it began to hit him.

Through all those layers of cynicism about churches and hypocrites came a call. At first he fought it. *I must be turning weak. This can't be the Lord. I'm imagining things.* But the call persisted, and Bernie knew that the One who was calling him was asking for more than a token surrender. He was asking for his life.

Only God and Bernie know how many weeks the inner struggle dragged on until one Sunday morning, there he was, next to Sonya, taking communion. For Bernie, this was not a ritual act. He was committing himself to Jesus all the way. As Bernie communed beside Sonya, he was joining himself to Christ's death, putting his old life behind him.

That was the day the Spirit began to move with power in Bernie's life. Today, seven years later, the life of God in this man is still on the increase.

There is only one level of Christian commitment: radical commitment. Commitment that requires us to put our hand to the plow and never look back, to leave the dead to bury their own dead and go out there with Jesus and proclaim the kingdom. "Lukewarm commitment" is a meaningless phrase.

Childlike Obedience to Jesus' Commands

Jesus kept placing before his disciples the example of a child. "Unless you turn and become like children, you will never enter the kingdom of heaven" (Mt 18:3). He was encouraging in them a spirit of childlike obedience: obedience to his word that simply accepts it and does it. If Jesus says, "Forgive," it forgives. If Jesus says, "Love," it loves. If Jesus says, "Believe!" it believes. It goes where it is sent and does what it is told.

Most of us lost that childlike approach to Jesus by the time we were seven years old. We were already learning to weigh the consequences of adult orders. If Mother asked us to wear something that would make us look weird in the eyes of our classmates at school, we balked. "No way! I'm not going to wear that!"

By the time we reached maturity, we were skilled at manipulating authority for our own advantage. "Yes, sir!" we would exclaim to the boss. "I'll have that taken care of by four o'clock this afternoon." But if we decided that the matter wasn't really as urgent as the boss was making it, we'd calmly place the order on the "maybe" pile.

Think of how many commands of Jesus you have placed on your "maybe" pile. For starters, consider these:

- "Love your enemies and pray for those who persecute you" (Mt 5:44).

- "Do not be anxious about tomorrow" (Mt 6:34).

- "Judge not" (Mt 7:1).

- "Forgive, and you will be forgiven" (Lk 6:37).

- "Give, and it will be given to you; good measure, pressed down, shaken together, running over, will be put into your lap" (Lk 6:38).

Jesus insists that unless we turn and become like children we will never enter the kingdom of God, because little children who trust their mothers do not have a "maybe" pile. They obey. And we are called by the Master to repent of our arrogance before the living God and become children before him.

Obedience and faith are twins that always travel together. If faith seems to be lagging behind in our experience, it is usually a sign that obedience has been neglected. Nothing builds faith (in those who have already heard the word) like obedience. Every command Jesus gives us is given in love—for our good.

Mending Broken Relationships

So if you are offering your gift at the altar, and there remember that your brother has something against you, leave your gift there before the altar and go; first be reconciled to your brother, and then come and offer your gift.

MATTHEW 5:23-24

In chapter eleven we will observe how a spiritual awakening always calls for obedience to Jesus in the area of forgiveness, and how when the Spirit moves with power, he becomes exacting about our need to reconcile. Revivals spread when we reconcile and fade when we refuse. Even at the outset, to prepare the way for the Spirit to ignite our hearts, we need to repair the broken relationship. "Leave your gift there before the altar and go; first be reconciled to your brother, and then come and offer your gift."

Not long ago Jean and I went to visit a friend in the hospital who had recently decided that his marriage was intolerable. He had walked out and moved in with friends from his cell group.

Now he was lying in a hospital bed, waiting for test results. Was the tissue malignant or benign?

While we were there, his wife surprised him with a visit. As she entered the room, the atmosphere became tense. There were shy spaces in the conversation, but beneath their reserve a spark was discernible. He was glad she had come, and so was she.

The four of us held hands and prayed, then Jean and I left them with each other. Two people who love Jesus and love each other were trying to take the first step toward healing the hurt in each other's heart. One could almost hear the Spirit of the Lord nudging them along, "Don't be afraid. Keep going. You're on the right track."

It comes down to this: are we thirsty enough for the fullness of God's Spirit to swallow our pride and reach out to that person on the other side of a broken relationship? We need to understand that if there is one person in our life from whom we are withholding forbearance or forgiveness, we are working against the very revival for which we pray and placing ourselves in a precarious position before the throne of God.

Make friends quickly with your accuser, while you are going with him to court, lest your accuser hand you over to the judge, and the judge to the guard, and you be put in prison; truly, I say to you, you will never get out till you have paid the last penny.

MATTHEW 5:25-26

Start Asking

Not long ago at a family dinner we were sitting around the table drinking coffee, when someone asked, "Where were you when you proposed to your wife?"

The men began to describe what they went through trying to "pop the question," and the women gave their versions. It was funny, but it was also moving. It caused us all to look back and remember one of the most important decisions of our lives. The men recalled what it was like to ask another human being to come into their lives for the rest of their days on earth. The women remembered thinking of the implications of such a momentous step: Does he understand the consequences for him if I say yes? Is he prepared to fulfill his part of this covenant?

Inviting the Holy Spirit to come in and take charge of our lives is like a proposal, only more so.

Sometimes we approach the matter of asking for the Holy Spirit like a man who proposes to a woman without grasping the import of what he is saying. "Will you marry me?" he asks. But he hasn't considered the changes her presence in his life will bring. It will mean that she will be there with him from now on, with a will of her own, views of her own, habits that may be different from his. Her moods will not always coincide with his. Nor will he be able to predict what she will think or how she will respond. He will no longer have just himself to consider when it comes to how he uses his time or where he spends his money. In fact, it won't be his time or his money any more, but theirs.

When we invite the Holy Spirit into our lives we are inviting another person into our lives—to stay. We are making a "proposal" of far-reaching consequences that will change everything in our lives. For the Holy Spirit has only one will: the will of the Father; one mind: the mind of Christ. He comes to set fire to our hearts. But this fire belongs to God, not to us. It takes charge of us, directs us on a new path and leads us to a cross as surely as the Spirit led our Master to a cross. If you are ready to make this proposal, then start asking.

> Which of you who has a friend will go to him at midnight and say to him, "Friend, lend me three loaves; for a friend of mine has arrived on a journey, and I have nothing to set before him"; and he will answer from within, "Do not bother me; the door is now shut, and my children are with me in bed; I cannot get up and give you anything"? I tell you, though he will not get up and give him anything because he is his friend, yet because of his importunity he will rise and give him whatever he needs.
>
> LUKE 11:5-8

Don't be discouraged if your "proposal" is not answered immediately. In the above parable Jesus is showing us that we need to make our "proposal" persistently. The man who went to his friend at midnight and pounded on his door got a bad reception.

We can picture one of our own friends treating us the same way. "Are you crazy? Coming to me in the middle of the night! Waking my kids! And then you expect me to get up and give you bread? Go on home, I'll talk to you tomorrow."

But we persist. We need the bread, and we know our friend well enough to believe that if we keep after him, he will relent and give us the bread we need. "Come on, Jack, I know you have bread in there, and I need it for my friend. I'm not going to let you have any sleep until you give it to me."

At last our friend gets up and gives us bread. Not because we're friends, but because we have badgered him.

More than once Jesus uses the example of someone who is relentless in pestering God for help. He presents the widow who hounds the unjust judge until she is vindicated as an example of how believers should "pray and not lose heart" (Lk 18:1). He teaches his disciples the value of tenacity as he "holds out" on the Canaanite woman who seeks healing for her demon-possessed daughter (see Mt 15:21-28).

Jesus encourages us to pester the Father for renewal in the Holy Spirit. The Father won't be upset. He desires to give us the Spirit far more than we thirst for him. But he waits. He lets us knock for a while. He gives us a chance to prove to ourselves that we're serious about receiving life from above. People who aren't urgent enough to become pests aren't urgent enough.

Keep "proposing." Keep asking. Jesus promises that if we ask, we will receive. But we have to ask with a heart that's pure enough, and urgent enough to keep asking.

What father among you, if his son asks for bread will give him a stone; or if he asks for a fish, will instead of a fish give him a serpent; or if he asks for an egg, will give him a scorpion? If you then, who are evil, know how to give good gifts to your children, how much more will the heavenly Father give the Holy Spirit to those who ask him!

LUKE 11:11-13

There is no such thing as approaching the Father for renewal in the Holy Spirit and being refused. This is a prayer that is always answered with a yes. Everyone who asks receives. Everyone. This is the gift Jesus came to give us. To make this gift available to us, he laid down his life. The fire of heaven is yours for the asking.

Have Faith in God

You are asking for the fullness of the Holy Spirit. And now you begin to live in expectation of the answer. You are certain that the Holy Spirit in all his fullness is about to follow the path you have cleared for him right into the center of your heart. Faith that this will happen is not a matter of how you feel about it. It is a matter of the will. Jesus commands you to trust God in this matter, so you obey.

> If you love me, you will keep my commandments. And I will pray the Father, and he will give you another Counselor, to be with you for ever, even the Spirit of truth, whom the world cannot receive, because it neither sees him nor knows him; you know him, for he dwells with you, and will be in you.
>
> JOHN 14:15-17

You may feel nothing, see nothing, experience nothing but your own yearning. Never mind. Keep asking. Keep believing. God is about to set fire to your heart, because you have demonstrated that you mean your "proposal" by preparing the way.

FOUR

The Spirit Takes Control

What happens when God sets fire to our hearts? John Wesley described how his heart was "strangely warmed." Dwight Moody looked back on an overwhelming experience of God's love that was so sacred to him he kept it a secret for fourteen years. The new disciples in Ephesus "spoke with tongues and prophesied" (Acts 19:6). But beneath whatever outward signs of divine fire in a person's life, the inner miracle is always the same: an invisible Person takes up residence within. "He dwells with you, and will be *in* you," Jesus promised, describing how the Holy Spirit would soon be the disciples' constant Counselor (Jn 14:17, emphasis added). He would direct them, no longer from outside, but from within.

Each of the four Gospels contains the same promise: "John answered them all, 'I baptize you with water; but he who is mightier than I is coming, the thong of whose sandals I am not worthy to untie; he will baptize you with the Holy Spirit and with fire'" (Lk 3:16).

Jesus' coming into this world, his ministry, his death, his resurrection—all were aimed at accomplishing this one miracle: to make it possible for human beings once more to be inhabited by the Spirit of God, as none had since the fall of Adam. For centuries the Spirit was active in this world, particularly among the people of Israel. He guided Moses. He spoke through the prophets. Yet, because of sin, the Spirit could not dwell in their hearts.

Then the Son of God emerged from his baptism to begin his ministry as the Son of Man, and the Spirit of God came upon him in fullness and to stay. Jesus proceeded to pioneer the way so that we could walk in his steps. By his death on the cross, he removed the curse of sin and made it possible for us to walk in righteousness by the power of the same Spirit which came to him. He wants us to carry within us the same power of God that anointed his lips and flowed through his hands.

In fact, Jesus made it clear that there is no other way. That which is born of the flesh is flesh. It cannot see or enter the kingdom of God. We have to receive a "new heredity," as Oswald Chambers called it. We have to have the nature of God himself placed within us so that the life of the Father and the mind of the Son literally begin to replace our old heredity of flesh and blood: "But to all who received him [Jesus], who believed in his name, he gave *power to become children of God*; who were born, not of blood nor of the will of the flesh nor of the will of man, but of God" (Jn 1:12-13, emphasis added).

The coming of the power of God is a supernatural event, which produces a supernatural change at the center of our beings. When the Holy Spirit takes up residence within us, we receive our new natures; we are adopted into God's family; and we inherit his character as his sons and daughters.

Our New Heredity

The shape of your face, the color of your eyes and the sound of your voice are manifestations of your family's hereditary line, which stretches back through generations and disappears out of sight.

But there is one characteristic we all have in common. We have inherited a predisposition to think and behave as if we were each the center of the universe. We have inherited a fallen and sinful nature. To think of ourselves first comes naturally. People around us become significant to the extent that they bring us joy or pain.

It isn't much fun being chained to ourselves. How often we wish we weren't so self-conscious. What a wonderful thing to be able to go through the day without constantly worrying about what's going to happen to us. Is that pain in my stomach gas or is there something growing in there? Why did Nancy duck down the other aisle as soon as she spotted me at the grocery store? Will I still have this job next year, or will there be another buyout? We can't help being fixated on ourselves. It's our heredity. Even when we turn over a new leaf and resolve that we're going to "live for others," we end up either as hypocrites or as nervous wrecks. We just can't break out of this mold of self-preoccupation. Until the Spirit comes.

And the Spirit does come. You've prayed for this miracle. You've prepared the way for it. And now he comes. The proof that his coming is happening is not that you are having a vision or that you have been struck down by blinding light or that you suddenly feel moved to open your mouth and prophesy. Praise God if you are experiencing such things. But the proof that the miracle is taking place is that you find yourself able, for the first time in your life, to actually obey Jesus. You couldn't before. But now you can. Another will has come alongside your weak will, setting it free to be able to joyfully obey the Master.

It's not your nature; it's Christ's nature living in you, and you find yourself able to do what you could never do before. Like a child growing into the likeness of his or her parents, you are now growing into the likeness of your heavenly Father, as the Lord Jesus helps you from within by the power of the Holy Spirit:

> For God has done what the law, weakened by the flesh, could not do: sending his own Son in the likeness of sinful flesh and for sin, he condemned sin in the flesh, in order that the just requirement of the law might be fulfilled in us, who walk not according to the flesh but according to the Spirit.
>
> ROMANS 8:3-4

This new heredity enables us to love God and to love people as we never could before. It is not a matter of resolving to "live for others." Our resolve (inspired by the Spirit) is to please the Father. As we fix our hearts on him, the Father enables us to live out of our new heredity. By the power of the Spirit we begin to change into the likeness of our Lord who came, not to be served, but to serve, and to give his life as a ransom for many.

Christ Jesus Is Formed in Us

Now the Spirit begins the work of sanctification—*forming us into the likeness of Christ*. This wonderful change does not happen in an instant. It is a process that requires our cooperation all along the way. As we yield to the Spirit's leadings and submit to his word of correction, our character begins to take on a striking resemblance to that of our Master. The love that has begun to burn in our hearts is not our love, it is Christ's love, imparted to us by the Holy Spirit. We are visited by a peace that passes understanding, a peace we did not inherit from our earthly parents; it belongs to our new heredity. The peace of Christ, now dwelling in us, is settling storms that have raged within our souls since childhood.

We find ourselves able to take hold of the Word of God with a faith that is new to us. It is the same kind of faith Jesus had when he calmed the Sea of Galilee and fed five thousand with five loaves and two fish. Now this faith lives in us, helping us to trust God as we were never able to before. We begin to experience a joy that is totally free of the circumstances around us. This joy is there in good weather and bad, when our stomachs are full and when they are empty.

As our minds are being renewed in the mind of Christ, who "emptied himself, taking the form of a servant" (Phil 2:7), we are set free to live without being distracted by the needs of our egos. We are doing what we're doing for Jesus, and not for the eyes of our neighbors and friends and critics. If someone else gets the "credit" for bringing Jack to church after we did the praying, calling and serving that prepared the way, may God's name be praised. We did it for the Master, not for some "audience." The Spirit is teaching us to serve God and not to let our left hand know what our right hand is doing. If the widow across the street never bothers to say thank you when we mow her lawn in the heat of the summer, we did it in Jesus' name. No thanks needed. With the mind of Christ, we seek to please the Father rather than to earn recognition from our friends and neighbors.

We Are Empowered to Walk in His Will

"If the Spirit of him who raised Jesus from the dead dwells in you, he who raised Christ Jesus from the dead will give life to your mortal bodies also through his Spirit which dwells in you" (Rom 8:11). It's like a resurrection. We rise from a death state, in which we just could not obey God's commands, into a life state where we can. Our mortal bodies are released into the freedom and power of the Spirit.

I don't know if my friend Mike would have described himself as a driven Christian, but he was certainly driven by a desire to help people. And many a person was helped by him. Yet the more he listened to the words of Jesus, the more troubled he became. Mike was honest enough to admit to himself that he did not have it in him to love his neighbor the way Jesus required it. And Jesus' insistence that his followers be reconciled with their brothers convicted him, when he considered all the loose ends in his own relationships that needed attention.

Then came hope. The promise that the Spirit would make it possible. Mike took hold of that promise with faith.

The old Mike died. The new Mike who rose out of his grave was washed in the blood and empowered by the Spirit. It was no longer Mike, but Christ. The commands of Jesus, which before had discouraged and disheartened him, became paths to fullness of life.

"It's amazing!" Mike would say. "I can do it now! Well, not I, but Jesus in me. It really works!"

The proof of whether the fire of God has reached our hearts is not that we saw a vision or spoke in tongues or prophesied, but rather that we are now able to do the impossible things Jesus commands us to do.

Working Out What the Spirit Works In

"Work out your own salvation with fear and trembling; for God is at work in you, both to will and to work for his good pleasure" (Phil 2:12-13). As he did with Mike, God puts the fire into us. And now comes the joyful task of "working it out," letting the Spirit manifest himself through practical changes in our living. We have a new heredity. Christ is being formed in us. We have been given power. And that power has now enabled us to make certain changes in our lives. The Spirit gives us all the help we need as we begin to develop transformed attitudes, renewed relationships, sanctified work and inspired disciplines.

Transformed Attitudes

Over the years we have developed attitudes toward others and toward life itself which belong to our old heredity. These do not automatically disappear when the Spirit enters our lives, as we quickly discover the first time someone offends us and that old venom spills from our mouths. Attitudes change only as we change them. The Spirit gives us the power to do this, but we have to make it happen.

Perhaps you are habitually irritated by people who like to drive slowly on winding, two-lane roads. Don't they ever look in their rearview mirrors? Can't they see that they have ten cars bottled up behind them?

But now you have a new passenger in your car, living within your own body. The Spirit in you calls for patience. Why are you working yourself into such a state over that driver's failure to accommodate you?

Here is a perfect opportunity to begin a change of attitude. As you ease up and fit in with the flow, the Spirit causes you to see how many other moments of your day are polluted with attitudes of anger, impatience and criticism. He helps you see how impatient you are with people who don't answer their phones in time, people who eat too slowly, think too slowly, walk too slowly. Ease up, says the Spirit. You are not the center of the universe, God is. Jesus loves these irritating people and died for them. Fit in with his program, and you won't be so obsessed with trying to make the universe fit into yours.

Maybe you're a habitual pessimist. Or perhaps puddles of bigotry have collected in the cellar of your soul. Many of us are just the slightest bit paranoid. We approach life with an attitude of enlightened suspicion. Everybody around us is guilty until proven innocent. Some of us are "Christian whiners," living in a chronic state of pious lamentation. The Spirit of God helps us to recognize that these attitudes exist in us and gives us the power to change them.

Usually when the Spirit makes us aware of an attitude that

needs to change, we deny it. How could you ever think that I wallow in self-pity? Please! But after being convicted a few times, we begin to get a glimpse of what the Spirit sees as he looks into our souls. And we know that if the miracle of revival is to proceed in us, we will have to take steps to change. What a joy to know that we are no longer imprisoned in this attitude! We can break free. We can replace it with an attitude that comes with our new heredity.

Renewed Relationships

Say your wife just let you know that she isn't happy about your inviting two couples over for dinner without consulting her. Now you're in the backyard having a little sulk, thinking of all the reasons why you shouldn't have married her in the first place, how you have put so much more into the relationship than she has. Why can't she be more hospitable? Of course, you don't know the first thing about preparing a meal, but it can't be *that* much work!

Out of nowhere two words come crashing into your consciousness. They are spoken softly, yet with an authority that frightens you. You've never heard the Holy Spirit speak directly to you before, but what else could it be? "Love her" is the gentle command. Nothing more. Suddenly you know that she is not in the wrong—you are. By inviting these guests without even considering her, when much work will be required on her part, you have demeaned your wife.

The Spirit is revealing to you, in this moment of self-pity, that your relationship with your wife is still part of your old heredity. It needs to be renewed. And it will be renewed, if you will obey his one command: Love her. You have been busy trying to make this woman fit into your program, but that is not your job. Your job is to love her. Love her just the way she is. Love her the way Christ loves his church. Fit in with her in Jesus' name, instead of forever expecting her to fit in with you.

When we committed ourselves to be disciples of Jesus, we understood that he was to come first in our lives, ahead of husband, wife, parents or children. "He who loves father or mother more than me is not worthy of me," says Jesus (Mt 10:37).

But commitment to Jesus is never license to take our spouses or our children or our parents for granted. While Jesus is to come first, ahead of every other affection, our relationship with others, especially those close to us, is to be ruled by the Spirit of love. Our spouses cannot be disregarded as we pursue the "interests of the kingdom." We each have a special kingdom responsibility for the person whose life we share. The Spirit of God has come to help us to bring all our relationships into the fresh new life which his love imparts, as we allow that love to flow through us.

Sanctified Work

"Man, I hate this job! I'd leave it in a minute, if I didn't have a family to support." With shrinking benefits, disappearing job security, the constant pressure to produce the most in the least amount of time, many men and women are at their wits' end in the workplace. They have to survive, but they wish there were some way to earn a living without draining their souls in this accelerating rat race.

The Spirit of God may not change your circumstances in the workplace, but he will certainly change you as he revives your spirit.

Work. We're stuck with it. Whether we're running households or driving semis over the interstate, cleaning teeth or designing software, most of us are tied down to a life of work.

We have often lived as though our work lives were something separate and apart from the kingdom of God. As if faith in Jesus is to be practiced in our off hours—when we go to church, when we shut the door behind us and pray, when we visit the sick and shut-ins. Yet our work, which consumes so much of our time and energy, is of major interest to the Spirit of God. The Spirit within us does not go to sleep while we go to work. He goes to work with us. He takes an interest in what we're doing and how we're doing it. He helps us in our relationships with the people around us. He is there to bring the kingdom of God into the workplace through us.

We bring the kingdom of God into the workplace by putting in a good day's work. The young man who was caught reading his Bible behind a pile of pallets on company time did not impress the foreman, when he explained that he was "having his devotions."

"I was witnessing until past midnight last night and was late getting up," explained the pious one.

"Stick that Bible back in your pocket and get to work," answered the foreman, "and if I catch you doing that again you're out of here!"

But we do more than put in a good day's work. We are an extension of the body of Christ in that office, factory, home, school, hospital or loading dock. Since we have been revived, we work with bodies that have become temples of the Holy Spirit. The life of God flows through us. People are encouraged, healed, given hope by our very presence in that place.

It is not an accident that we are working in the place where we are. We have been sent to this place by the Master himself (unless we're printing counterfeit money or refining heroin, in which case the minute the Spirit of the Lord gets hold of us, we know it is time to switch careers), and he commands us to let our light shine. All we need to do is practice his presence, and those long, monotonous hours of work will be sanctified. God will use them for his purpose. The flame of revival will burn even there.

Inspired Disciplines

To stay fresh over the long haul, there are certain habits the Spirit of God will help us to practice. These habits or disciplines were present in the life of our Lord, when he lived on earth. No follower of Jesus can survive without them. Our personal revival is only complete as it results in the formation of these disciplines: prayer, a lively use of the Bible, participation in the life of the body of Christ, faithful handling of money, a life of service.

Prayer. At the beginning of your personal revival, prayer is usually the easiest thing in the world to do. Prayer just comes bubbling up from within. You love to pray. Your time alone with God is the most refreshing hour of the day. But be forewarned:

your honeymoon with prayer will be followed by a season when you will wonder whether the spring has dried up. What went wrong? Did I take a forbidden turn? Why has the luster gone out of prayer? Why has prayer, which was once such a joy, become so difficult?

Nothing went wrong. Your Red Sea celebration is over, and now it's time to plunge into the wilderness, where you learn to pray even when prayer is difficult. In chapter eight we will examine how prayer is essential to sustain revival in our personal lives and to spread revival beyond ourselves. But for prayer to have the place in our lives that the Lord Jesus commands it to have, it must become a discipline—a thing we make ourselves do on a daily basis, whether we're in the mood for it or not.

The Spirit helps us to pray and guides us in our prayers (see Rom 8:26), but we have to do the praying. My friend Glen always says that you can only steer a bicycle when it's moving. The Spirit of God can only steer our prayers when we're praying. The Spirit's job is to flood our prayers with the life of God, to intercede for us with "sighs too deep for words" (Rom 8:26). Our job is to keep praying day after day, in season and out of season, so that the Spirit can do his job.

A lively use of the Bible. The Bible is our "handbook of revival." As we will see in chapter five, the Bible, which has played a pivotal role in every revival, is preserved for us by God, to help us stay fresh and on track. But this record of God's words and actions can only help us if our use of it is lively and regular. By lively I mean that we do more than cover so many chapters a day. We think. We listen. We pay attention. We ask the Spirit to show us what we need to see as we read it.

And our use of the Bible needs to be disciplined. The Bible is not God, but it is the place where we meet God. The Bible is not Jesus, but it is the place where the crucified and risen Lord Jesus comes to meet us and speak to us. The Bible now speaks to us in a way it could not speak before we were indwelt by the Holy Spirit. Now the Spirit, who inspired Moses and the prophets and burned white-hot in the ministry of our Lord, confirms to our hearts the things we read. But we have to read. We have to discipline ourselves to come to this book daily with alert minds and listen to what it has to tell us.

Participation in the body of Christ. There is a difference between casual participation in the body of Christ and disciplined participation. Casual participation means that I go when I feel like it, making sure that church doesn't interfere with my personal life. Disciplined participation means that I commit myself to serving Jesus in the context of this particular body of believers. I will worship with them every week, except when I'm sick or out of town. (If I'm out of town, I'll find a body of believers somewhere and worship with them.) I will get to know these people. I will open my life to them. I will serve them.

For most of us, disciplined participation in the body of Christ includes being part of a small group within the larger fellowship. It could be a Bible study that meets in the church or in someone's home each week. Or a prayer group. Or a combination of the two. If there is no small group, you may find yourself helping to gather one, with the approval and guidance of the church's leadership. The revival that is working in your life is also at work in the lives of others. You will find these people, and they will find you. Together you will commit yourselves to serving that church with a spirit of strong encouragement.

Faithful handling of money. To his disciples, Jesus said: "He who is faithful in a very little is faithful also in much; and he who is dishonest in a very little is dishonest also in much. If then you have not been faithful in the unrighteous mammon, who will entrust to you the true riches?" (Lk 16:10-11).

Often we have thought that we were handling money, when in fact money was handling us. We worried about it, lost sleep trying to figure out how to increase our hoard of it. Or we dreamed about how nice it would be if we *had* a hoard of it. Mammon became our master. Jesus has made clear that if we allow mammon to be our master, it will be impossible for us to serve God. And now that the Spirit has entered our lives with power, one of his primary goals is to set us free from our bondage to mammon. He comes to teach us to truly seek first the kingdom of God and to trust that the heavenly Father will indeed provide for us.

Jesus never said that money was unimportant. We never hear Jesus say, "Money means nothing to me." Jesus teaches that money, the "unrighteous mammon," is actually the trial material by which we prove that we are capable of handling the riches of the kingdom. Until we are able to handle money faithfully for God, we are not ready to be entrusted with the powerful riches of God's Spirit. The Spirit will help us to be faithful to God in our handling of money as we engage in disciplined giving, disciplined generosity, and disciplined management.

"Disciplined giving" means that we prayerfully decide on a percentage of our income that we are going to slice off the top of every paycheck and put into "God's bin." It's all very well to say that all our money belongs to God, but we will continue to use it as though it belonged to us until we take a meaningful portion and give it away as an offering to God. The money that we put into "God's bin" may be passed on to our church, and perhaps to a missionary, or to an organization that feeds the hungry or cares for children. The Spirit will help us decide where, beyond our local church, some of this money should go. We give, not because the church needs money, but because we need to give as an act of continuous thanksgiving and praise to God.

"Disciplined generosity" means that, over and above our tithe (whether it's ten percent or more or less), we train ourselves to be aware of needs that require our help. "Give to him who begs from you, and do not refuse him who would borrow from you," said Jesus to men who were already tithing their income (Mt 5:42).

We hear of a flood in Colorado or a famine in Korea or thousands of families displaced by a localized war in Africa, and we hear the Spirit saying, "You can help." So we send a check to the agency of our choice.

Often the needs are close to home. A neighbor has been laid off for the third time in two years. His family needs help. We train ourselves to manifest to this man and to his family, with our money, the same kind of generosity the Lord God has shown to us.

But aren't there times when we really need to say no? As my friend Haskell always says, "Don't worry about learning how to say no, until you've first learned how to say yes." Generosity is not part of our old nature. It comes with our new heredity, but we only learn it through practice, through discipline.

"Disciplined management" means that we train ourselves to manage our financial affairs as stewards of the kingdom rather than people who answer only to themselves. We buy and sell and save and spend, remembering that we are making these decisions under God.

One time our friend Lucille came into a large sum of money. When she spoke with Jean and me about it, she sounded as though she wished this burden had not been dumped on her. "What should I do with it?" she asked, almost hoping that someone would tell her to sign it over to some worthy cause.

"The Lord put it into your hands because he knows he can trust you, Lucille. He'll show you how to handle it. Meanwhile leave it where it is and keep living for him."

In the years that followed Lucille managed that money like a steward of heaven. She was generous but not gullible. She used it as she used her very life: to serve God by quietly helping people.

We may not have as large a "problem" dumped on us as Lucille had. But we are equally responsible before God to manage what comes into our hands in a way that pleases God.

A life of service. Martin Luther once said, "Love God, and do as you please," meaning that if we truly love God, we will be driven by a desire to please him. What higher pleasure can there be than to please the one we love?

Yet old habits have developed such deep grooves in our behavior patterns that, without discipline, we find ourselves constantly sliding into the familiar grooves. None of us, after receiving the fullness of the Spirit, suddenly becomes a joyful, self-giving servant. This is what we want to be. But it won't happen until we begin working out, in daily living, the spirit of servanthood which God has put into us. We have to discipline ourselves to do what does not come naturally to us, until it becomes natural.

This discipline takes place in two areas: our bodies and our minds. We begin by presenting our bodies to God as living sacrifices, as the apostle Paul counsels us in Romans 12. Daily we offer our bodies to God to be temples of his Spirit so that the will of Christ Jesus may be accomplished through these hands, these feet, these tongues. We commit ourselves to worshiping God with our bodies all day long. Then we go forth into the day, remembering that our bodies belong, not to us, but to our Lord.

> Do you not know that your bodies are members of Christ?
>
> 1 CORINTHIANS 6:15

> Do you not know that your body is a temple of the Holy Spirit within you, which you have from God? You are not your own; you were bought with a price. So glorify God in your body.
>
> 1 CORINTHIANS 6:19-20

This means that the Lord is going to do the Father's will, using our bodies, even while we're sorting laundry, fixing cars, making beds, answering phones, driving down the freeway. He is going to help, encourage, strengthen, heal people, using our bodies. Our role in this miracle is simply to keep presenting our bodies to the Father as living sacrifices. The Lord's role is to turn our bodies into sacraments, manifestations of his presence in the real world, as we go about our lives.

The second part of this discipline of service is to continuously choose not to be conformed to the spirit of the world around us, but to be transformed (as Paul explains in Romans 12) by the renewing of our minds. So that allowing our thinking to be lifted daily and hourly into the mind of Christ, we can manifest God's redemptive will in this troubled world through simple acts of service: "Have this mind among yourselves, which you have in Christ Jesus, who, though he was in the form of God, did not count equality with God a thing to be grasped, but emptied himself, taking the form of a servant" (Phil 2:5-7).

We discipline ourselves to think like servants. By the power of the Spirit we translate the servant-mind of Christ into our daily planning, the practical decisions that need to be made, hour by hour.

When our daughters were in their teens, they were caught up in a revival that was visiting the youth of Detroit and many of its churches. The clearest evidence to Jean and me that our daughters' hearts had been touched was that their teenage self-preoccupation was strikingly transformed into servanthood. Our son, who was eight years old at the time, was so impressed with his sisters' new approach that he began to imitate it.

What's going on? we wondered. Is this for real?

It was. They had found spiritual renewal and, with no small amount of effort, were training their minds to think like servants.

Personal revival, for the first time in our lives, brings us the power to live in this world as servants of God and of each other. The Spirit who lives in us is the Spirit of servanthood. He imparts to us the very mind of Christ. Now comes the joyful task of turning our new heredity into flesh-and-blood living by disciplining ourselves to think and act like servants.

FIVE

Staying on Track: Using the Handbook of Revival

Once we have begun to experience the joy of spiritual renewal, we need to make sure this new surge of life continues to move in the direction God intends it to take. The Spirit has come into our lives for a purpose far beyond anything we can imagine. He wants to use us in his redemptive plan, to spread the heavenly fire through us to others.

But our old heredity keeps rearing its head and wants to divert the revival into a program of its own. Perhaps I get taken up with this "good feeling" that revival has brought and sail off on a "feeling tangent." I compare how I feel at tonight's prayer meeting with how I felt last week. I wonder whether I am feeling the presence of God as strongly in my prayers today as I felt them yesterday. Or I narrow spiritual renewal to one "movement" or church (the one I belong to), looking upon all other movements or churches as inconsequential.

To protect us from the danger of being carried off on a tangent and losing our way, we are given the Bible. It is not an accident that the Bible holds a prominent place in every spiritual awakening that has ever occurred among the people of God. The Bible keeps us on track. It warns of the dangers that lurk beyond that beam of light God sheds on our path, and it clearly guides our steps. Once we have experienced revival we are more dependent than ever on the witness of Scripture. Revivals—personal or corporate—that lose touch with Scripture quickly lose touch with God.

Jesus opened the Bible in his hometown synagogue and read from Isaiah 61. "'The Spirit of the Lord is upon me, because he has anointed me to preach good news to the poor....' He closed the book, and gave it back to the attendant,... and he began to say to them, 'Today this *scripture* has been fulfilled in your hearing'" (Lk 4:18, 20-21, emphasis added).

With that reading of Scripture Jesus introduced to Israel a revival such as it had never known. The blind received their sight, and the lame began to walk. Hearts were turned to God. Lives were changed. Most important of all, a band of disciples was gathered who would soon change the course of history. Jesus took pains to make clear to his followers that this revival was based on Scripture. He had come to fulfill Scripture. "And beginning with Moses and all the prophets, he interpreted to them in all the scriptures the things concerning himself" (Lk 24:27).

The spiritual awakening that exploded on Pentecost took its first big leap forward as Peter opened *Scripture*. "Men of Judea,... these men are not drunk as you suppose, since it is only the third hour of the day; but this is what was spoken of by the prophet Joel: 'And in the last days it shall be, God declares, that I will pour out my Spirit upon all flesh'" (Acts 2:14-17).

It is not an accident that we find Scripture playing a prominent role in every revival the Spirit sends. Revivals are the fulfillment of Scripture. They are the manifestation of the life of God that the Scriptures promise. When we experience personal revival, we are invariably drawn to the Bible and are nourished by it. If our personal revival is to continue to sustain us, we will need to allow the Bible to keep us on course. Without the counsel of Scripture, we are prone to veer from the path of discipleship without knowing it. The Bible is the handbook of revival and is meant to be our constant companion as we walk in the Spirit.

The Bible played a major role in my personal revival. By the time I completed seminary, my respect for Scripture had been weakened by the form critics. Which Isaiah was the real Isaiah? Who really wrote the book of Hebrews?

Four years later, when our new congregation had been organized in Dartmouth, Nova Scotia, and our building program had been completed, I began to ask myself a few questions, like, is this all there is to the kingdom of God—a church full of decent people whose hearts, like my own, are wrapped up in a thousand distractions? Where is the presence of God in all this? Where is the power to transform our lives? The answers were in that book lying on my desk, but I didn't know it.

During summer vacation Jean and I stumbled into a church in Reading, Pennsylvania, that was far from that to which we were accustomed. "Where the Healing Waters Flow," flashed the blue neon sign on the roof. We could hear singing as we came in. People were clapping to the beat. Hands were raised. The place was alive with joy. Pastor George spoke with an authority I knew I lacked. So I swallowed my pride and asked him to come over to Nova Scotia while he was vacationing in Maine. He smiled and said he'd "pray about it." Sure. We'll see.

Two months later Pastor George and his wife came. The Holy Spirit came with them. I can still remember the ending of Pastor George's prayer: "Answer the cry of this young man's heart!" And that prayer was answered almost instantly. Call it fire from heaven. Call it the baptism of the Holy Spirit. All I know is that the Spirit of God took hold of me with a grip that has never loosened in all the years since.

Jesus became far more real to me than he had been before. Prayer began to rise from my heart with a freedom and confidence which were totally new. And the Bible came to life. Suddenly the things I was reading about in Scripture described what I was actually experiencing. God does speak. The Spirit does lead. Those healing waters of apostolic days are still flowing.

I don't know if the words were any different when I preached, but the results were. People came under conviction. They began making changes in their lives, as I was making changes in mine. I invited people to come together to study the Bible. And they came, hungry to think and share and pray as the Spirit opened the Word to us. The Bible literally became our handbook, as the Spirit worked his work of revival among us.

"Something has happened here since I visited last year," said Bill, my preacher friend who came up from New Jersey. "These people are changed. You are changed. What is it?" Everything Pastor George had given to me I passed on to Bill. He took the "fire" with him to his home in New Jersey, and soon his people too were experiencing revival. And they, like we, found themselves drawn to the Scriptures. The Bible became their handbook.

This kind of spiritual awakening is presented in Scripture as perfectly normal, the kind of thing we should expect wherever Jesus is obeyed. Revival occurred everywhere Paul went. Paul spoke under the unction of the Holy Spirit, and people came to faith. Their lives were changed as the fire of revival spread through the grass roots.

Yet from these earliest days revivals have tended to flare up and fade. So often the brilliant early days of spiritual awakening are followed by long seasons of dull orthodoxy. Churches that were once on fire with passion for the Lord Jesus content themselves, a generation later, with venerating the spiritual giants of their revival days. Sometimes revivals that start out well "jump the track" and roar off on a tangent of excess that everybody—except the participants—seems to recognize as excess. God has given us a handbook to show us how to stay on course and stay fresh. All we have to do is use it.

The Bible is simply the witness of men and women over centuries of time who encountered the flame of God's presence in their lives, welcomed it and obeyed it. Abraham met God. Hagar was visited by God. Moses stepped onto holy ground and didn't even know it, until God told him to take off his shoes. The witness of these people has been preserved for one purpose: to lead us into communion with the same God who spoke to them, to ignite in us the same flame that burned in them. But we have to take the plunge and join them by disciplining ourselves to read this book and learn what they have to tell us.

Personal Bible Reading

If we want to make sure our spiritual awakening doesn't veer off on an unhealthy tangent, a discipline of personal Bible reading is essential. We need to set aside a period of time each day to be alone and become familiar with everything that is in this book.

Begin in the New Testament. Read the Gospels—Matthew, Mark, Luke and John. Always be open, as you read, for a word the Spirit may want to address to you. About forgiveness, perhaps. Or the command to have faith. "Do not fear, only believe" (Mk 5:36) may come just at the moment you need to hear those words. God will help you decide how many chapters to cover each day, but it will probably be at least one. Don't just wet your toes, jump in! Immerse yourself. Pause, once in a while, and listen, or talk to the Lord about what you're seeing and hearing as you read these words.

From the New Testament Gospels read on into Acts and the Epistles. But don't wait too long before adding some Old Testament reading to the New. Genesis, Exodus—wonderful books! They lay the groundwork for the rest of the Bible. Soon you may be ready to memorize some psalms to help you with your praises and to sustain you through difficult days. Use whatever Bible-reading guides you find helpful. But discipline yourself to read this book daily.

Group Bible Study

As the spiritual awakening spread through our church in Nova Scotia, we began to get together to study the Bible. In the very beginning we would sit in the church for half an hour in total silence. Then we'd gather in a room and take the book of Luke, a paragraph at a time, and talk and share. Later we opened the study time with singing and praise. Intentionally these Bible studies were kept informal. People were free to talk about their personal needs in the light of the Scripture we were covering.

Informal Bible study, where nobody is an expert and everybody is open and teachable, as believers search together for a clear word from God, is a practical way of allowing the Spirit to nourish us and guide us. Unless we sink our roots deep into the Scriptures, the joy of revival will be blown away by the first major storm that comes sweeping into our lives.

We study the Bible together to help each other become the kind of men and women Jesus is calling us to be. "For I tell you, unless your righteousness exceeds that of the scribes and Pharisees, you will never enter the kingdom of heaven" (Mt 5:20). Our righteousness is to exceed that of the scribes and Pharisees, and the scribes and Pharisees were no slouches. They put extreme effort into trying to live up to the law. In his Sermon on the Mount (see Mt 5, 6 and 7) Jesus tells us exactly the kind of people we are to be, by the power of his Spirit. We come together and ponder his words and encourage each other to translate them into living.

As we study the Bible alone and together, we need to approach it, first, with eyes that look beyond the letter; second, with ears that are open to a fresh word from the Lord.

Eyes That Look Beyond the Letter

Jesus came to restore wine to the wedding feast of Israel. But at every turn he was opposed, harassed, slandered and threatened. He described his persecutors: "You blind guides, straining out a gnat and swallowing a camel!" (Mt 23:24).

Who were these men who gave Jesus such a hard time? Bible students. The scribes and Pharisees spent long hours in their houses of study poring over Scripture texts, consulting the ancient commentaries, considering every possible meaning for a single word or a phrase that could be interpreted seven ways.

What they learned in their long years of study failed to prepare them for this Galilean who healed the sick and cast out demons and turned the temple into an uproar. "He can't be of God," they murmured. "He breaks the Sabbath and eats with sinners."

Going by the letter of Scriptures, like ecclesiastical prosecuting attorneys, they pronounced Jesus guilty of major sins. Using Scripture, they found every reason to demand his death. Because they never saw beyond the letter.

From the earliest days of the church Christians have fallen into this trap. They have mercilessly persecuted Jews, fought bloody crusades, burned each other at the stake over points of doctrine and used Scripture to justify their deeds. They found words in the book that could be made to say what they wanted them to say. "His blood be on us and on our children!" (Mt 27:25). Isn't that what they answered Pilate on Good Friday? So let's get 'em!

Walls of suspicion that divide believers from one another are built from words taken from Scripture and twisted to mean what the divine Author never intended.

How can this happen? Jesus gives us the answer: "You search the scriptures, because you think that in them you have eternal life; and it is they that bear witness to me; yet you refuse to come to me that you may have life" (Jn 5:39-40).

If we fail to follow the Scriptures to the One to whom they bear witness, or if we try to use Scriptures apart from a relationship of obedience to Jesus, they become for us a "written code" instead of the living Word. And a written code always kills; only the Spirit gives life (see 2 Cor 3:6).

Our personal revival has given us eyes that are able to see beyond the written code to the One to whom the Scriptures point. Nit-picking time is over. It's time to act on the one message that Scripture gives to all who have eyes to see: "Turn to me and be saved, all the ends of the earth" (Is 45:22). "Come to me, all who labor and are heavy laden, and I will give you rest" (Mt 11:28). The message, from Genesis to Revelation, is simply "Come." And the voice we hear is the voice of the Shepherd himself. As long as we are in these bodies of flesh and blood, we keep coming to him who is the source of our hope, the goal of our journey. We come to him through the Scriptures that renew our minds to behold him and that teach us how to obey him.

Open Ears

Morning by morning he wakens,
he wakens my ear
to hear as those who are taught.

ISAIAH 50:4

It's not enough to see. We see to be able to hear. Meeting the Master in the Scriptures, we begin to hear his voice. "The hour is coming, and now is, when the dead will hear the voice of the Son of God, and those who hear will live" (Jn 5:25). The moment we begin to hear, we come to life with the life of God. And as we act on what we hear, the life of God in us increases. On the other hand, if, once we hear, we turn away from what we're hearing, a darkness that begins to invade our souls is far worse than the darkness of ignorance.

Sometimes words seem to leap off the Bible's page and cry out to us. Sometimes impressions nudge us in a direction we've been hesitant to take: repentance of an attitude, a phone call to a brother with whom we need to be reconciled, an anonymous gift to a neighbor in need. Sometimes a word of awesome comfort comes to us. "Lo, I am with you always, to the close of the age" (Mt 28:20).

The Bible is the history of the Shekinah glory descending to earth and igniting human lives. This glory manifests itself throughout Scripture as fire. Holy fire. Cleansing fire. Fire that conveys the presence of God.

- When Adam and Eve were expelled from Paradise, a "flaming sword which turned every way" guarded the way to the Tree of Life (Gn 3:24).
- God's covenant with Abraham was confirmed with a "smoking fire pot and a flaming torch" passing between the pieces of Abraham's sacrifice, evidence that God was present, confirming his promise (Gn 15:17).
- Moses encountered God at a bush that was on fire (see Ex 3).
- The Israelites were led through the wilderness by the Shekinah, a cloud of glory which by night became a fire in the sky (see Ex 13:20-22).

- When Moses dedicated the tabernacle, "fire came forth from before the Lord and consumed the burnt offering" (Lv 9:24).
- Elijah's prayer was answered with fire from heaven (see 1 Kgs 18:36-38).
- Fire hovered above the gathered believers on Pentecost, broke into tongues and came to rest upon each of them (see Acts 2:1-4). The Shekinah glory, resting on ordinary Jews—not a priest among them—was a sign that God's love was being shed abroad in their hearts by the Holy Spirit.

Now the fire has come to us. God's Spirit burns in us, a living flame, for a purpose far greater than our minds can grasp. We have been brought into God's revival. To keep the flame within us fresh and constant we have been given God's own Word of Testimony, the Bible. If we will use it, allowing the Spirit to guide us as we read, this priceless book will keep us alive and on track throughout our earthly journey.

PART TWO

Use Me for Your Glory

SIX

Let Your Fire Spread

The wonderful new sense of communion with God, the joy and the gifts that have come to you through your revival, have a purpose far higher than your personal fulfillment. Thank God for that fulfillment, and know that the flame of God's Spirit burning within you is a foretaste of glory waiting beyond this world. But also be certain of this: God has put his Spirit in you so that he can use you in ways that surpass human comprehension. He has poured life into you so that it may overflow to others. Are you ready to let this happen?

God is giving you the privilege of being part of his redemptive plan on earth at this hour, a plan which is already in motion. The Spirit has ignited a revival on this earth which many believers are hoping will be the last and the greatest. He is causing it to spread. This revival is developing according to the Spirit's agenda, but there is one part of its expansion in which you have a say:

Are you willing to let the fire spread through you? You can say yes, or you can say no. If you say no, God will raise up someone who will say yes, for his revival will spread. If you say yes, God will use you in ways that will stagger your mind.

You will discover that the most important things in God's kingdom usually take place away from the spotlights and TV cameras. The significant miracles rarely occur in pulpits or on church platforms. God's kingdom makes its power felt at the "street level," where people actually live: in the workplace, the bus stop, the coffee shop, the kitchen, the backyard. In such places you will find yourself touching lives with the healing power of Christ. It will happen in such ordinary ways that you will hardly be noticed. But these lives will be affected for all eternity—through you.

Who, me? you may be inclined to say. How can God possibly use me? God did not make a mistake when he revived you and called you to be his servant. The Lord Jesus plans to accomplish supernatural things through you.

When the Spirit of the Lord calls a man or woman into his redemptive purpose, he seems to pick the person who feels unqualified. "You must be mistaken, Lord. What do I have to offer?" Moses protested that he had a speech impediment. Gideon insisted that he was the least in a clan that was the weakest in Manasseh. Mary was "greatly troubled" when the angel Gabriel said, "Hail, O favored one, the Lord is with you!" (Lk 1:28).

If you find it hard to believe that the Lord is calling you to be a means by which he ignites others, you're in good company. The people God uses are invariably those who have no confidence in their own powers—so they will have to rely on his. And he gives them a promise: "I will be with you."

The God who called you into this revival will empower you to serve it. Here's how it works. First, God will locate you, if he hasn't already, in a place in the body of Christ that could use some encouragement. I said at the beginning of this book that every genuine revival in an individual leads to cleansing and increased life in the body of Christ. In this case, you are the individual. And your personal revival is now about to spread beyond you.

By way of preparation for this miracle, pretend for a moment that you are a member of the church at Laodicea in Revelation 3. This church was very successful by all the standards we are inclined to use to measure success. The crowds were good and the money was coming in. Yet, beneath the surface, this church was in trouble; its connection with heaven was, in Jesus' words, "wretched, pitiable, poor, blind and naked" (v. 17). Oh, it was a busy place. It had found the secret of success in compromise. It gave people what they wanted, the promise of blessing, without the need for radical commitment to Jesus. "You don't have to be a fanatic to be part of this church. Come and be blessed in our relaxed, easy atmosphere!"

You are a member of this thriving Laodicean church—this church with an empty soul. You open your Bible to Revelation 3:20 and read these words directed specifically toward your church: "Behold, I stand at the door and knock; if any one hears my voice and opens the door, I will come in to him and eat with him, and he with me" (Rv 3:20).

Jesus is calling your church to repentance by addressing the individual: "...if *any one* hears my voice and opens the door...." The key to revival in this spiritually lifeless church is the man or woman who is willing to answer the Master's knock and let him in. One person responding to the Master's knock will open the door to revival for the whole church.

The key to spiritual ignition in your Laodicean church is *you*. You don't have to organize a thing. It doesn't begin with preaching or teaching or programs or meetings. Whether you are the pastor or the forgotten soul in the last pew, there is one thing you need to do—the only thing within your power to do: open the door. Open the door to Jesus on behalf of that church. He will come in and eat with you, and as you commune together, he will cause the flame he has already placed within you to spread.

The church in which God actually locates you may not have any of the characteristics of the church at Laodicea. It may not be thriving numerically, as the church at Laodicea was. Or it may be weighed down with discouragement, distracted by the changes going on in the world around it. Or it may be a typical contemporary American church, striving to grow and keep up with the times. Whatever the case, you will begin to discern needs, needs that will be answered by the flame within you, as you keep opening the door to the Master's knock.

A Vision of Service

God will give you a vision of what he desires to do for that church.

Often we see ourselves as people who have all we can do to survive the changes that are swirling around us. Our jobs are on the line, and bills have to be paid. The children need to be driven to music lessons, ball games, church activities. We are weary, short of time, haunted by the relentless pressure of the workplace. Who's the next person to have the chair pulled out from under him or her? Will it be me? Even the older ones among us are frequently like Martha in the kitchen, "anxious and troubled about many things." Everybody is struggling to function in a hard-edged world.

But when we look at ourselves with eyes of the Spirit, we become sheep for whom the Shepherd has glorious plans. He is about to transform these harassed sheep into a kingdom of priests. God gives us vision, and a new vista opens before us. We see ourselves as part of a fellowship of believers where the presence of the Spirit of God is so real and so strong that people are lifted out of their fears, delivered from their weariness, energized by the breath of heaven. Everybody still has to go to work every day, and pay bills and drive the children to ball games and music lessons. But the Shepherd who once seemed so indistinct and distant has become the burning center of their lives.

In your vision you will see the Spirit quickening the worship life of these believers. Breath from another world begins to revive them as they give thanks to the Master who is making them whole. You will see reconciliation spreading through the assembly as the Spirit of the Lord calls the people into unity around himself.

Your vision expands into the places where the people of this church go through the week, carrying the healing power of Christ into the shop, the office, the school, the neighborhood. You watch them pass on the healing Jesus gave to them. They're having coffee with neighbors, going bowling with old friends, listening to colleagues at work. They're on the phone. Someone is sliding an envelope with some money in it under the door of an old woman down the hall who paid her rent and has nothing left for food. You are watching supernatural changes taking place in the congregation as the Spirit of God comes to rest with power upon its people.

Empowerment for the Vision

God will empower you to fit into the vision. When God gives you a vision, it is always because you are somehow connected with the vision's fulfillment. You are being shown what God intends for his church, and you are being made to know that you are part of the program. As you fit into the program, God will use you to make it happen.

For instance, the only reason Mary came to Jesus and announced, "They have no wine," was that Mary already had a vision of this faltering wedding feast restored to life (see Jn 2). She saw in her mind's eye what would happen if her son, Jesus, revived this feast. And she knew that she was to fit into this vision. Her job was to step up to her son and tell him, "They have no wine."

Jesus seemed displeased. "O woman, what have you to do with me? My hour has not yet come." But Mary refused to be rebuffed. She held firm in her faith that Jesus would restore this feast somehow.

"Do whatever he tells you," she said to the servants, and returned to the feast.

"Fill the jars with water," said Jesus. The servants filled six stone jars used for the Jewish rite of purification.

"Now draw some out, and take it to the steward of the feast."

The steward tasted the wine and announced to the baffled groom, "You saved the good wine until now! This is excellent!" The wedding feast came to life as joy and laughter filled the rooms. The disciples watched all this and knew that they were witnessing a sign of the kingdom. And it began with one woman fitting into her vision.

You fit into your vision by discerning the needs around you and responding as the Spirit leads you. A stranger comes to church and no one seems to notice her as the service ends. Her clothes are out of style. She appears to be working up the nerve to press through the crowd at the door and get out as quickly as possible. Yet you know that some need brought her here. Surely she cannot be allowed to slip out without receiving a welcome. Wal-Mart would treat her better than that. So you walk over to her and smile and open your mouth, hoping that the Lord will give you a few helpful words. You speak, and the woman's troubled face relaxes.

Many of us have grown up with the idea that the real work of the kingdom is done by pastors and missionaries. Or at least by people who play some prominent role in worship. After all, what can I do for God, just sitting here in this pew?

But the real work of the kingdom begins when our worship time ends. In corporate worship we offer ourselves to God in thanksgiving and praise. His Word speaks to us. His Spirit refreshes us. Then we leave the assembly and scatter into the everyday world, where God turns us into broken bread and poured-out wine for the people around us, just by being there. Just by doing your sick neighbor's laundry or changing a tire for the elderly stranger whose wheel went flat in front of your house. Or picking up the phone and calling someone whose name crossed your mind as you were praying this morning. "How are you? Haven't seen you for a while." That's all you need to say, and a conversation begins that brightens this person's day and imparts hope.

As we perform these simple acts, responding to the needs

that come our way, two things are happening: life is flowing from the cross of Jesus, through us, into the world; life is also flowing from the cross of Jesus, through us, into the body of Christ. Every time we serve people out in the world in Jesus' name, we are not only conveying life to them, we are being used by the Spirit to strengthen the body of Christ. The body is edified as its people obey the Spirit.

New Life

You will see life burst forth, as people ignite with hope.

> The seventy returned with joy, saying, "Lord, even the demons are subject to us in your name!" And he said to them, "I saw Satan fall like lightning from heaven. Behold, I have given you authority to tread upon serpents and scorpions, and over all the power of the enemy; and nothing shall hurt you. Nevertheless do not rejoice in this, that the spirits are subject to you; but rejoice that your names are written in heaven."
>
> LUKE 10:17-20

Some of the best things that are accomplished through our lives will be hidden from us until the Day of the Lord. "Lord, when did we see thee hungry and feed thee, or thirsty and give thee drink?" (Mt 25:37). In his mercy, God often allows us to bring his life to others so unconsciously that we don't even know we're doing it. Perhaps our egos couldn't handle too much "kingdom success." But to encourage us, the Lord always permits us to see at least a glimpse of the joy that comes to people who take hold of the hope we hold out to them. We watch them open their hearts to receive Jesus into their lives. We see the fire spread. We see men and women and young people coming out of the shadows of unbelief and taking the places God has prepared for them in the spreading revival.

You will see hearts ignite because of the hope you bring them. Encouragement will dawn on their faces because you came to them in their troubled hour and stuck with them throughout the storm. People who were afraid to trust you, because they had been let down so many times, will begin to lay aside their cynicism and fall in step at your side. And the fire within you will leap across to them. You will see revival spread to others through you.

Don't be discouraged if it takes a bit of time. The revival spreads at the Spirit's behest, not ours. Twelve years seemed almost like an eternity to me, as I and others with me kept praying for revival to come to our inner-city church in Detroit. Messiah Church had been standing at the corner of West Grand Boulevard at Toledo Avenue for more than half a century. During that time the neighborhood had changed, the city had refashioned itself, but the church was still there. In the twelve years since I had come from Nova Scotia to be its pastor, Messiah Church had experienced numerical growth and financial increase, but spiritually it was like Elijah's sacrifice, still waiting for fire from heaven.

A handful of us shared this concern in our Bible studies and times of prayer together. We knew that God had something more than we were presently experiencing. And we knew that if this church were to have an impact on the neighborhood for the kingdom of God, it would have to have much more power.

We introduced healing services. We began meeting the first Friday of the month for all-night prayer. Some of us fasted. The congregation continued to grow, new faces mixing with the old and adding some color to the assembly. But we knew this church still lacked the life-transforming power it needed. The gifts of the Spirit, and especially the fruits of the Spirit—love, joy, peace—were still in short supply.

Our prayers for renewal were answered in a surprising way. I had come to the conclusion that part of the problem was that this church was still clergy-dominated. And I was the clergy-man. Talk all you want about the priesthood of all believers, many folks like the idea of being the "laity." "You take care of the spiritual things, Reverend, and we'll look after the building and count the money."

"How would you feel if I took a year off and got a job in the Cadillac plant?" I said to my wife, Jean. "I'd continue to preach on Sundays and lead Wednesday night Bible studies. But I'd take no salary and all the other work would have to be shared by the whole congregation."

It was fine with Jean. Fine with our four children. Not so fine when I broke it to the church council. I held my ground, and the council gave its grudging consent. I sent a letter to the congregation three weeks before our annual meeting, inform-ing them of the new plan.

Pandemonium. Anger.

Who does he think he is?

The most troubling concern among the older members was, Who's going to bury us if we die?

It was time to back off. At the annual meeting I agreed to continue as pastor. "If you die before I do, I'll bury you, but

I'm no longer going to function as chaplain to a religious club. I'm going to be out on the streets and in the bars reaching out to people with the gospel. And if that doesn't work, I'll leave this institution and open a storefront down on Vernor Highway."

The people who had been praying for renewal were with me in this. They were already sharing in the ministry of Messiah Church with their prayers and their witness within the church and beyond it. These people were not a clique. They related well to the larger body of the congregation. But they had a vision of the kind of life that God wanted to give that church and were trying to fit into it.

It hardly looked as if revival was on the way. Attendance dropped. Even the furnace seemed to balk at this "rocking boat" and treated us to a cold church one February Sunday. We kept on praying. And in March, for some inexplicable reason, attendance began to climb. New faces turned up out of nowhere. Then came Palm Sunday. That was the day, after twelve long years of praying and waiting, the answer came. I ended the sermon with an altar call, an unheard of thing in the tradition of Messiah Church. People streamed forward. As they were praying the fire fell. Messiah Church ignited, and the flame has been burning among these people ever since.

What do you mean, Messiah Church ignited? I mean that from that day, and for the next eighteen years at Messiah Church, I never had to think of myself as a chaplain to a religious society again. People were igniting with the fire of the Holy Spirit, and the fire was spreading. The atmosphere had changed. Radical commitment to the person of Jesus was no longer considered fanaticism. It was looked upon as the norm.

It was what we all desired and pursued.

I went out on the streets and into the bars, as I had promised. I'd park the car along Vernor Highway (the "main drag" of the neighborhood) and start walking. In the bars I received a welcome more often than not. And in the local park there were plenty of people to talk to and listen to. Soon I was no longer doing this alone. Others came out to "work the streets." On Saturdays it became a regular practice for a group of us to meet for prayer at one o'clock and then "go fishing."

Wednesday evening Bible study, which for twelve years rarely exceeded fifteen souls, began to swell. Within a year the numbers had multiplied tenfold, and we had to move the meeting into the church, where it has been ever since. But numbers don't tell the whole story. Numbers may fluctuate as the Spirit gathers and sifts. The proof that the fire of heaven had fallen on Messiah Church was threefold:

First, our relationship with Jesus came to life. I began to hear people talking about Jesus as if they knew him. They were no longer ashamed of the name Jesus; it was their joy. Jesus was the Vine, they were the branches, delighted and awed to be drawing their life from him.

This new relationship with Jesus became evident in the worship life of the congregation. Whether it was liturgical worship on Sunday mornings (often interrupted by spontaneous prayer) or "free" worship on Wednesday evening, there was a strong awareness of the presence of the Lord. The assembly was wrapped in an atmosphere of thanksgiving so clear that strangers who came to visit were embraced and held by it.

More than once visitors would declare as they left the service, "The Lord is in this place."

People who had never had a prayer life began to discipline themselves to spend time alone with God each day. Praying. Listening. Reading Scripture. Interceding. And for those who already had a prayer life, prayer became a new thing.

Out of these disciplined prayers came changes in the way people lived. One young man reported to us that he was AWOL from the army, and he was shown in prayer that he would have to turn himself in. He did his time, received his discharge and was soon with us again. Debts were paid. Enemies were reconciled. Work habits were improved. But the driving power behind it all was the fire of heaven, bringing our relationship with Jesus to life.

Second, our relationship with one another came to life. We began to live out the words of Jesus:

> A new commandment I give to you, that you love one another; even as I have loved you, that you also love one another. By this all men will know that you are my disciples, if you have love for one another.
>
> JOHN 13:34-35

We began to see kindness in places where it had been lacking before. People were reaching out to each other, caring for one another in a new way. A young man needed a car to get to work. Someone else in the fellowship came through with a car for him. Old folks were treated with special deference by the young. People who had only seen each other in church for years were now getting to know each other.

The sick were visited. Families in financial straits were helped, often without even tapping the church's benevolence funds, which also were beginning to flow more freely. Somebody would hear about a need and take care of it without a word. Never before had Messiah Church seen generosity practiced so freely and joyfully. The Spirit of God was moving hearts.

Third, our vision of the harvest came to life. We began to understand as a congregation that God had brought us together in order to reach out beyond ourselves. Within a four-mile radius of our building was a rich mission field made up of people from no less than thirty nations. We knew that we were commanded to go "to the streets and lanes of the city, and bring in the poor and maimed and blind and lame" (Lk 14:21). We found Lazarus at our gate in a hundred forms. Addicts and prostitutes were not strangers, they were our friends and neighbors. Clearly, the Lord wanted them also to become our brothers and sisters.

As we reached out, the Spirit sent in reinforcements. Young families from the suburbs began attending our gatherings. Many of them took the plunge and moved into the neighborhood to help with outreach. We didn't have to go overseas to find the Third World. It was right in front of us. And it was ripe for harvest.

Revival at Messiah Church began and continues because people allowed their personal renewal to spread outward. If you are willing, the revival which has come to you will spread outward through you. "I came to cast fire upon the earth; and would that it were already kindled!" said Jesus as he set his face toward Calvary (Lk 12:49). That fire is now burning—in you. It wants to spread. It wants to bring the power of the kingdom of God to bear on many lives—through you.

SEVEN

Give the Spirit Room

We now return to a truth we learned when the Spirit first set fire to our hearts: the fire could only enter us as we made room for it. The Spirit of God cannot enter you if you are full of yourself. The Spirit can only dwell in a person who has cleared the way, as we observed in chapter three. But this lesson that we learned in our personal revival applies with new force and broader dimensions as God uses us to spread revival to others.

Have you ever considered why Jesus chose you to be one of his disciples? Did he look out over the vast sea of humanity and say to himself, Ah, there's a person with talent! Just what I'm looking for!

That's the way they do it at General Motors and NBC. They want talent. They scrutinize your qualifications. They evaluate your personal appearance. But when it comes to calling people and putting them to work in his kingdom, Jesus doesn't seem to do it the way they do it at GM and NBC.

Look at the twelve men Jesus chose to be his apostles. What seminary would accept a man like Peter? His clothes smelled of fish, and his beard was never trimmed. Thomas was always raising questions. Philip—what could Philip put on a resumé? Jesus chose his apostles, after an all-nighter in prayer, satisfied that the Father was directing him to choose, not the "wise and understanding," but "babes" who were teachable.

Think of the woman God chose to be Jesus' mother. Mary lived in one of the most backward towns in Israel. It is hardly likely that she could read or write. But Mary knew how to yield to God's will. "Behold, I am the handmaid of the Lord; let it be to me according to your word" (Lk 1:38).

Paul summed it up this way:

> For consider your call, brethren; not many of you were wise according to worldly standards, not many were powerful, not many were of noble birth; but God chose what is foolish in the world to shame the wise, God chose what is weak in the world to shame the strong, God chose what is low and despised in the world, even things that are not, to bring to nothing things that are, so that no human being might boast in the presence of God.
>
> 1 CORINTHIANS 1:26-29

The Lord Jesus looked out over the sea of humanity and saw you struggling, weak, troubled, confused, and said, "Here's a person who might give me room to work in his [or her] life." He did not choose you because of your talent or good looks or celebrity status, but for the opposite reason. He chose you to be a sign of what grace can do in a human life.

Once we have been chosen, we begin to learn the principle of remaining empty, a lesson we keep learning the rest of our lives on earth. "Blessed are the poor in spirit, for theirs is the kingdom of heaven" (Mt 5:3). The poor in spirit are the people who are empty of themselves. They have come to a place where they no longer rely on their own wisdom or skill or righteousness. They have nothing. They come to God with empty hearts, crying out to be filled with his forgiveness and peace: "Behold, as the eyes of servants look unto the hand of their masters, and as the eyes of a maiden unto the hand of her mistress; so our eyes wait upon the Lord our God, until that he have mercy upon us" (Ps 123:2, KJV).

Our personal revival began when we divested ourselves of every claim on God but his mercy. No matter how many prayers we prayed, or how many tears we shed, or how much tragedy we lived through, or how many days we fasted, or how much we sacrificed, we found that our only claim on God was the cross of Jesus.

Yet many of us still carry within us the secret belief that God is fortunate to have us in his service; that we bring with us into the kingdom a rare integrity, a sincerity that outdoes the competition by a mile; that our insights are a valuable asset to God's program on earth, and we are pleased to make them available. Surely God owes us something in return for our faithfulness through all we have suffered!

Revival can only spread through us as we repent of all spiritual fantasy and become children before the heavenly Father.

Charlie Daniels was a regular at our all-night prayer meeting the first Friday of the month. Most of us were young. Charlie was old. He had seen his share of trouble in his seventy-nine years, but he knew where to turn for help. When the rest of us were struggling to keep awake and pray, Charlie was up at the rail, pleading with the Lord. His words still ring in my memory: "Comin' to ya, Lord, 'cause we need ya! Comin' to ya, Lord, 'cause we need ya!"

What else do we have to offer the living God but hearts that are empty and need to be filled again and again with his Spirit? (As we see in Acts 4:31, the believers who had been filled with the Spirit on Pentecost were filled afresh as they cried out for boldness.) Our heart's cry must be: Lord, help me to empty myself of the self-righteousness, and the self-confidence and the self-pity that clutter my heart, so the fire you have given me may burn clearly and spread through me to others.

The first gift the Welsh Revival brought to people was a spirit of brokenness. People were on their faces before a holy God. They confessed their sins and cried out for mercy. They saw themselves, for the first time, in the light of God's searching holiness and repented of what they saw.

The second gift of the Welsh Revival was joy. Once they emptied themselves before a holy God, the Spirit filled these believers with more joy than they could contain. It overflowed in rivers of thanksgiving and praise and transformed living. Joy came to them as they became empty—poor in spirit—before the Lord, and lived in them as they remained empty.

The revival God sends into our personal lives is no different. Its first blessing is to impart to us a spirit of brokenness. The Spirit lovingly convicts us of the immense load of spiritual baggage, which before was a source of such pride, but now is seen for what it is: clutter, vanity, sin. We begin to empty ourselves so God can fill us with his life. "God, be merciful to me a sinner!... Lord, I'm not worthy to have you come under my roof; just speak the word ...."

Then the Lord Jesus reaches down and lifts us up. We are flooded with the power of his cleansing blood, the peace that only that blood can bring. God breathes into us the breath of his Spirit, and we rise and stand on our feet, ready to serve him, like Ezekiel's dry bones restored to life.

Even when we go forth to serve under the anointing of his Spirit, God still requires us to remain empty. "Take nothing for your journey," says the Master, as he sends us to serve in his spreading revival. "Discipline yourself to rely on nothing but me. I alone am your strength."

Going forth empty is often frightening, since we have been trained to approach every problem from a position of strength. Don't start building a house, we were taught, unless you have enough funds to complete the job. Don't take on the armies of the enemy unless your armies are superior.

But Jesus puts a new twist on this teaching. He says the strength we need to accomplish things in his kingdom does not come from within but from above. And to obtain strength from above we have to divest ourselves of our own "strength." "Whoever of you does not renounce all that he has cannot be my disciple" (Lk 14:33).

In other words, God can only use you when you're empty. This applies to all whom God uses to ignite his church with the fire of heaven. When we're full, full of ourselves, full of our knowledge or skill or wealth, the Spirit of God has no room to move in us. Our tendency to rely on the force of our personalities, our wealth of knowledge, the skills that have made us successful in our trades and professions, makes it difficult for us to yield to the direction of the Spirit.

Likewise, our churches, like the synagogues and the temple of Jesus' day, are often driven by the efforts of men and women of exceptional talent. Talented preachers draw crowds, talented musicians enhance the worship. Astute managers plan ahead for larger facilities. People come forward with their skills and gifts, and the church seems to thrive.

But before the Spirit of God can ignite any assembly, large or small, with the fire of heaven, he has to find someone who is open to Jesus' teaching about remaining empty.

Why did Jesus tell the young man who had "great possessions" to sell it all, give to the poor and follow him with empty pockets? Why did Jesus explain to Nicodemus, who had great knowledge as a teacher in Israel, that he would have to be born again? Why did Jesus repeatedly insist to his followers that whoever exalts himself will be humbled and whoever humbles himself (empties himself of "glory") will be exalted? Because it is only when we are empty of ourselves and lose our lives in him that the life of heaven can move through us.

There is wonderful comfort in this teaching. It means that every one of us can qualify, no matter how wise or how foolish we are. Whether rich or not so rich, young or old, plain or attractive, we can all enter the vision of a revived people and watch that vision come to life under the Spirit's power. All we have to do is give the Spirit room to work in us.

Jesus' Example

Theologians call it "the doctrine of the kenosis," the Eternal Word emptying himself of his glory to ignite a dying race with the fire of heaven.

> Who, though he was in the form of God, did not count equality with God a thing to be grasped, but emptied himself, taking the form of a servant, being born in the likeness

of men. And being found in human form he humbled himself and became obedient unto death, even death on a cross.

PHILIPPIANS 2:6-8

In this state of emptiness, divested of his divine prerogatives, willingly separated from the glory that was rightfully his, the power of the Father could move through the Son to open the door to Paradise which had been closed to us for so long. Never in his entire life on earth did Jesus do anything from his position as God the Son. He did it all as the Son of Man, totally emptied of his glory, utterly dependent on the Father for every need—his food, his shelter, his protection. His words were not his own; they came from the Father. His deeds were never self-motivated; they were acts of obedience to the Father. His power was the power of the Holy Spirit moving through his emptiness.

Jesus was no wimp. He stood before Pilate without fear. He rebuked the scribes and Pharisees with words that smoked. Demons feared him. The storm obeyed his command. Water froze beneath his feet when he chose to walk on it. But the power he commanded came from above and moved through him, because he was empty.

"Not my will, but thine, be done," he prayed to the Father as the cross loomed before him (Lk 22:42). It was the most difficult thing he would have to do. But to bear away the guilt of this sin-sick race, it would have to be done. He was yielded. He was empty of himself. So that when he bowed his head and yielded up his spirit, the earth shook, the veil of the temple tore apart, and the curse of Adam was broken.

Following Our Lord's Example

We give the Spirit room by "declaring bankruptcy," turning over everything we are and have to the Master. Dying to ourselves, we form the discipline of beginning each day by emptying ourselves of our "glory" and presenting our bodies afresh to the Master as a living sacrifice. Daily we clear our minds of the clutter of self, so that they can be renewed once again by the Spirit of God. How can the Spirit fill me, if I'm already full of myself?

How can the Spirit lead me, if my soul is a boiling pot of complaints, regrets, resentments, cravings and fears? I need to yield them to the power of the cross, so that they can be drained away in the Lamb's blood. Deliver me from myself, O Lord. Wash away the chaos within me and restore me to the peace you gave to your first followers when you came to them alive from the dead.

God will give us the wisdom we need. But only we can empty ourselves to receive that wisdom. "Take nothing for your journey, no staff nor bag nor bread nor money...." That is, "Make yourself dependent on me. Empty yourself of those things that might become your confidence in place of me. Put your trust in me alone, and I will use you in ways that surpass human thought."

I'm indebted to a man named Ralph, who helped me to see the importance of being empty. Ralph didn't talk about it; he just seemed to be aware that God had a program, and it was his job to fit into it—empty. Over a two-year span of time, Ralph was at the center of a move of the Spirit in Detroit whose effects are still evident, twenty-five years later, in many lives and numerous churches.

I met Ralph about six months after he arrived in town from California. By this time his following was a growing hodge-podge of university drop-outs, Vietnam veterans, high-school kids, street people and recovering addicts.

But how did it all get started? What did Ralph do when he arrived from the West Coast? Did he put up posters? Did he line up speaking engagements? Commercials on Christian radio?

No, he just sat in a park with his Bible and waited for further orders. He was empty. From conversations I had with those who were there, it happened something like this:

It was summertime and the park was an oasis of green in a grimy city. Mothers were walking their toddlers down the shady paths. Couples were strolling by the pond. Old folks lined the benches, enjoying their coffee and the morning paper. Off in a corner of the park, where the earth sloped up toward a mammoth oak, was the "market" where the dopers transacted business. Sitting on the grass, his back resting comfortably against the trunk of the ancient oak was a stranger dressed in worn army fatigues. His beard flowed to his chest, almost hiding the Bible that rested on his lap. At first nobody paid attention to him. He could be a narc, hiding behind that Bible.

The next day he was there again, sitting under the oak with the Bible in his lap. And the next day and the next. He didn't preach. He didn't initiate conversation. He waited.

On the fifth day Smilin' Dog, a well-known dealer, walked over to the man with the Bible.

"What's happenin'?"

"Not much."

"I seen you here the last four days. You gettin' ready to preach?"

"No."

"What's your name?"

"Ralph."

"You believe what's in that Bible?"

"Yep."

"Tell me about it."

The next day Smilin' Dog brought three friends. They sat on the grass and talked with Ralph about the Bible, about Jesus. Ralph told them that Jesus is coming soon.

Soon there were a dozen disciples. Then fifty.

When fall came and the weather turned cold, Ralph ministered to a flock of several hundred in a rented house. And it all began with Ralph sitting under an oak tree with his Bible, empty and waiting. The only thing Ralph was sure of was that he was to be there. He had no orders beyond that. Ralph obeyed what was clear to him and trusted that things would unfold in God's time. All Ralph had to do was fit in with God's program.

We approach our calling in a similar way. If the Spirit of God is going to use us to ignite our church, the first thing we have to do is simply be there—empty. Be content to be an empty vessel in the house of the Lord.

Who knows how long those water jars were standing in the house before Jesus ordered the servants to "fill the jars with water." But they were there, empty and waiting, when the moment came. If Ralph had sat under the oak tree every day for the whole summer and received no response, he would have kept coming. Ralph knew that he was to be there, and he believed that in time things would begin to happen. What would happen, how it would happen, when it would happen, was left to God. It was God's program, not Ralph's. Ralph was fitting in by simply being where he was supposed to be.

The Power of the Cross

Every believer open to being used redemptively by the Spirit of God soon learns that there is a price. While salvation is a free gift, paid for by the blood of the Lamb, those who yield their lives to the Lamb are crucified with him. To come out from the curse and live in the power of that cross, we not only have to accept Christ's atonement as a deed done, we also have to allow the power of that cross to work in us. "I have been crucified with Christ," says Paul. "It is no longer I who live, but Christ who lives in me" (Gal 2:20). Jesus not only died *for* me, he drew me into his death, so that dying with him to my own will, I might rise with him into the will of the Father. This means that we die to our own rights, ideas, principles, visions—so that Christ's life can flow through us as quickening fire to others.

The power of the cross of Jesus working in you releases the fire:

Always carrying in the body the death of Jesus, so that the life of Jesus may also be manifested in our bodies. For while we live we are always being given up to death for Jesus' sake, so that the life of Jesus may be manifested in our mortal flesh. So death is at work in us, but life in you.

2 CORINTHIANS 4:10-12

If we are willing to take hold of the cross and let the power of Christ's death work in us, we become a channel that carries a two-way flow. The fire of the Spirit's life flows out of us with healing and cleansing power into the lives we touch. At the same time the burden and the sickness and the sin that weighed upon these lives flows through us into the cross. As we keep one hand on the cross and the other on the person in need, we become that person's connection with the living Christ.

However, if we lose touch with the cross ourselves, while still holding on to that person's need, we become a receptacle for their burdens and will sink under the weight of them. We were not meant to be receptacles, only channels. Or if we keep holding to the cross, but fail to reach out to other lives, the flow of the fire through us will cease. Since the Spirit never remains stagnant, he simply goes looking for another channel.

Each of us needs to have the attitude that no one in this church is more needy than I. "The saying is sure and worthy of full acceptance, that Christ Jesus came into the world to save sinners. And I am the foremost of sinners" (1 Tm 1:15). We approach the task of letting our fire spread, not as heroes, but as sinners who have no claim on God but the cross of Jesus. Apart from his grace we are as lost as any human on this earth. Apart from him we have no goodness, no wisdom, no health, no authority.

When Daniel cried out to God to restore Jerusalem, he identified with Jerusalem's sins. Daniel did not stand aloof, but prayed as one who was part of the problem. "To thee, O Lord, belongs righteousness, but to us confusion of face.... For we do not present our supplications before thee on the ground of our righteousness, but on the ground of thy great mercy" (Dn 9:7, 18). In like manner we join ourselves in spirit to the hardest hearts, the most flagrant hypocrites in the church, and we say to the Lord, who knows the truth about us, "Lord, I am more needy than they. Cover my sins with your blood. Raise me out of the darkness of my own soul into your light."

It's God's kingdom. God takes the initiative. God sends the fire. Yet he has chosen to use you in his program, as he visits this world with life. Join yourself to the Lamb of God. Take hold of his cross and cling to it, until the power of his death delivers you from yourself. Then open your heart and let the fire spread.

EIGHT

New Dimensions in Prayer

"And in the morning, a great while before day, he rose and went out to a lonely place, and there he prayed" (Mk 1:35). Jesus was often in prayer, and we need to follow his example.

Nowhere is the work of the Holy Spirit more evident in our lives than in prayer. We experience a progression as the Spirit moves us from a starting point, where *we* are at the center of our prayers, to a place of usefulness, where *God* is the center. How rapidly we progress depends on us. Are we listening for the voice of the Spirit as we pray? Are we learning? Are we obeying?

The progress from self-centered praying to God-centered praying takes place in four stages:

Stage one: a personal crisis. Most of us experienced our first taste of the mercy of God in answered prayer when we reached a point of desperation.

For example, my friend Pat was feeling so low, she couldn't pray. So she asked a stranger to pray for her. One Sunday morning Pat was so beside herself with anger and frustration that she jumped into her car and just started driving. As she roared down Michigan Avenue, she wasn't sure she wanted to go on living in this absurd world. She had no idea why she turned right on Vinewood and slowed down at a gloomy railroad underpass. She noticed an old man filling his bag with empty cans for the deposit money.

Pat pulled over and rolled down the window. "Sir, can I ask you something?"

Pat is white. The stranger was black.

He approached her car and answered, "Yes?"

"Do you believe in prayer?" she asked.

"Yes, I believe in prayer."

"Will you pray for me?"

"What's your name?" asked the stranger.

"My name is Pat."

"I'll pray for you, Pat," said the man. He turned and went back to his cans.

Pat drove around the corner and parked on Toledo Avenue. The first thing she noticed was that her burden had lifted. The anger and frustration and hopelessness had mysteriously left her for the first time in many days.

The next thing she noticed was our church, directly across the street from where she was parked. She noticed on the sign that there was a Bible study on Tuesday mornings at 9:30, and decided that, since this was the closest church to where the miracle happened, she would come on Tuesday morning and share her story. It was then that we all met Pat for the first time.

Pat's faith blossomed. Soon she was praying, not only for herself, but for her family and a host of others.

A serious prayer life begins, for most of us, with a personal crisis. We find ourselves in a situation where all human help has failed, and turn to God in our desperation. A door opens and we have our first living encounter with the God who answers prayer.

Not only did Jesus answer the cries of those who came to him with their sickness and sin, he also promised that his heavenly Father will always give good things to us, if we but ask him (see Mt 7:11).

Stage two: prayer for personal revival. We enter this stage when we begin to appreciate the God who answered our crisis prayers. Recognizing those answered prayers as signs pointing to a loving Father, we begin to follow the signs until they guide us into the Father's presence.

For example, while Jesus' miracles were signs pointing to the kingdom, the men and women who were healed were under no obligation to follow the sign. Nine of the ten cleansed lepers took their healing and hurried back to the world that had been closed to them during all their years of suffering. Only one leper followed the sign to the one to whom it pointed. Likewise, many people who receive answers to their "prayers of desperation" never see these answers as signs that point to something far more wonderful. Like the nine lepers hurrying on their way, these people are content to remain at stage one. Their next serious prayer will coincide with their next serious crisis.

But those who recognize an answer to a crisis prayer as the sign of a loving Father who has much more to offer begin to follow the sign. Lord God, I want to know you. Set my heart on fire, so that I can clearly hear the voice of your Son Jesus, and follow where he leads! Bring me into the fullness of your kingdom! Use me for your purposes!

The prayer for personal revival, as we have seen in chapter

three, is prayer for a fresh outpouring of the Holy Spirit, a prayer that is always answered. Anyone who knocks on heaven's door and keeps knocking will receive this gift: "If you then, who are evil, know how to give good gifts to your children, how much more will the heavenly Father give the Holy Spirit to those who ask him!" (Lk 11:13).

Stage three: a crisis in the lives of others. I have a friend named Bill, who answered what he was sure was a call from God, and ended up as a teacher among the Masai tribes in Tanzania. Bill never claimed to be a biblical scholar or a theologian. Many times he would ask himself, What am I doing here? What do I have to give these people? Yet Bill was certain of one thing: he was there to serve them.

Bill may have been the most unconventional missionary these Masai tribesmen had ever seen. But they liked him and accepted him with his bulging blue eyes and his unkempt hair and the streams of sweat ceaselessly pouring down his flushed face.

A drought visited, and the herds were beginning to suffer.

"If your God is so good, why don't you ask him for rain?" they said, half in anger, half in hope.

"I will," answered Bill. What else could he say? How could Bill explain to these people that it wasn't that simple? Bill knew he was no Elijah, but he seemed to have no choice. His Masai friends were standing there, waiting for him to pray to his God. Bill lifted up his heart and his voice to the God who had led him out to Africa and asked him to answer his friends' cry for rain. Within thirty minutes the sky grew dark, and then came a long downpour that drenched the earth and revived it.

No one was more awed by this sign of God's love than Bill himself.

The tribesmen were grateful for the rain. But Bill brought them more than rain. The atmosphere of another world—God's world, God's kingdom—washed over these tribesmen like that shower and softened their hearts to the word that was coming to them through their friend, Bill.

When people bring their needs to us, and ask us to pray, it is a sign that God is drawing us close to the destination of our prayer journey: intercession. "Pray for me," they say. "I'm going through a crisis at work." Or, "My marriage is in trouble." Or, "I received bad news from my doctor." What else can we say, but yes! Even though we may feel utterly inadequate, even though we know that they are overestimating our spiritual maturity, our answer is yes. And now we are under obligation to keep our word to them.

Which brings us to the fourth and final stage in the progression.

Stage four: we begin to join our will to the will of the Father. To join our will to the will of the Father involves a disciplined prayer life in which we come to prayer, not so that God can enter into our purpose, but so that we can enter into his. The Spirit helps us make the transition from our purpose to God's purpose as we allow Jesus to be our teacher.

Go into your room and shut the door and begin with Jesus' own words in Matthew 6:7-10:

And in praying do not heap up empty phrases as the Gentiles do; for they think that they will be heard for their many words. Do not be like them, for your Father knows what you need before you ask him. Pray then like this: "Our Father who art in heaven."

The first thing we need to do—and the Spirit always helps us—is to lift our minds away from ourselves and our concerns and fix them on the Father who is in heaven. That is, he is our true Father who loves us with unspeakable love. And he is at the throne of all power. He is in control. I may be praying alone, but I am not alone. I am part of the family of the redeemed children of God on both sides of the grave who call him Father. He is *our* Father.

"Hallowed be thy name."

To say "Hallowed be thy name" is to say, "I'm taking off my shoes before your majesty, Lord God. I bow in awe to your glory." Think about it. Take your time. You are in the presence of the living God.

"Thy kingdom come."

I've spent a lifetime building my own kingdom (and calling it yours). Now I turn my heart away from my kingdom. I repent. And I cry out for your kingdom to come in its fullness to this earth, and to me. I present myself in submission to your kingdom and to its authority over all things.

"Thy will be done, On earth as it is in heaven."

I pray, heavenly Father, for your redemptive will to be done on this earth. That the blind may receive their sight, the lame walk, the lepers be cleansed and the deaf hear. That the dead may be raised and the poor have the gospel preached to them. Raise up laborers for the harvest. And may your holy and healing will be done in me and through me.

There needs to be a daily discipline of submission to the Father's will in prayer, just as our Lord himself repeatedly withdrew into the presence of the Father to be renewed. Many patterns have been recommended for this daily time alone with God. The Spirit will no doubt help you develop your own. But whatever structure your private prayer may take, there are three essential ingredients: praise and thanksgiving; listening; intercession.

Praise and Thanksgiving

The first thing the Samaritan leper did, after he discovered that he was healed, was to give praise to God with a voice that echoed through the hills. Then he came to Jesus, threw himself at Jesus' feet, "giving him thanks" (see Lk 17:11-19).

It is a good practice to follow that man's example of expressing appreciation. Enter into God's gates with thanksgiving and into his courts with praise. If you are having trouble praising God in your private prayers, open your Bible to the book of Psalms. Read aloud Psalms 95 to 100. Let the Spirit of the Lord soften your heart toward God as you join the numberless multitude on both sides of the grave who are lifting their hearts in praise to God. Angels, who never cease to give God praise, will come to your aid and push the spiritual cobwebs from the room so that your praises will rise more freely. And remember, as you praise God, that you are not doing him a favor. You are giving God his due.

The twenty-four elders fall down before him who is seated on the throne and worship him who lives for ever and ever;

they cast their crowns before the throne, singing,
"Worthy art thou, our Lord and God,
to receive glory and honor and power,
for thou didst create all things,
and by thy will they existed and were created."

REVELATION 4:10-11

Listening: Waiting for Guidance

Prayer is not a one-sided conversation. It involves listening.

The God who holds the universe together by the word of his power is not given to shouting. His voice is more likely to be heard as a whisper, as Elijah discovered on Mount Horeb. To hear that whisper we need to become still, not only with our mouths, but with our hearts. "Be still, and know that I am God. I am exalted among the nations, I am exalted in the earth" (Ps 46:10).

The Father will make his will known to you as you wait in silence before him. He will bring to mind people who need your attention. He will put his finger on areas of your life that need repentance. He will speak a word of hope, just when you thought there was no way out.

To wait in silence before God is not as easy as it may sound. Our minds like to "gather wool." They will ramble into the past, and tiptoe into next week and try out three scenarios for how things will go when we have lunch with that testy client. When we reminisce or daydream we are not being still before God, we are indulging ourselves.

Remember that when you are sitting or kneeling there in

silence, you are in the presence of One who knows you better than you know yourself. He has heard your appeal to him and has drawn near through the Spirit to listen and to speak. When you speak, he listens. When he speaks, you listen.

Intercession

One Sunday evening I went with "Sister Lee," an eighty-year-old servant of God, as she conducted her weekly ministry at the Wayne County Jail. This tiny little saint in her long blue dress and peaked cap grabbed the bars and said to the men milling around behind them, "Young men, I've been talking to you about Jesus, and you aren't listening to me. So now I'm going to talk to Jesus about you. He'll listen!" That was not meant as a threat, but as a promise to intercede. And intercede she did. Intercession was her specialty. Lee understood that intercession is the primary ministry of every Spirit-anointed follower of Jesus. Intercession is meant to be your specialty and mine.

And intercession is work. Never think that because salvation is a free gift, the life of following Jesus is without effort. The Lord who paid for our salvation with his own blood calls us to come under his yoke and learn from him. We learn as we work at his side. Yes, his yoke is easy, compared with all the other burdens we have tried to carry. But once we are under that yoke, even while our souls find rest, our bodies and minds are engaged in work. And the major work they perform is intercession.

I'm talking about private intercession, praying for people before the face of God alone. There is an important place for corporate prayer, followers of Jesus coming together to "agree on earth" about things they lay before the Father. But beneath all corporate prayer is the Spirit's call for men and women of faith to get alone before God and lift up the needs of the body of Christ, of Israel, of individual saints, of stumbling prodigals, to the Father, who has mysteriously tied his redemptive movements to the prayers of his people.

Moses interceded for Israel: "Alas, this people have sinned a great sin; they have made for themselves gods of gold. But now, if thou wilt forgive their sin—and if not, blot me, I pray thee, out of thy book" (Ex 32:31-32). Time and again Moses stood in the gap between a holy God and a rebellious people.

The Spirit of intercession runs through the whole history of Israel. Every prophet was an intercessor. Jeremiah wept before God for his people. Isaiah urged intercession on everyone who cares: "You who put the Lord in remembrance, take no rest, and give him no rest until he establishes Jerusalem and makes it a praise in the earth" (Is 62:6-7).

And Jesus sets an example of intercession for all his followers. The night of his betrayal, Jesus said to Peter, in front of the other apostles, "Simon, Simon, behold, Satan demanded to have [all of] you, that he might sift you [all] like wheat, but I have prayed for you [Simon] that your faith may not fail; and when you have turned again, strengthen your brethren" (Lk 22:31-32).

There was a time in my life when, though I had a disciplined prayer life, I never considered intercession to be a priority. I was satisfied that every believer is given a small bundle of people for whom to pray. All we have to do is pray for our little bundle. So I would pray for my family, some friends, a few leaders in the congregation I was serving and some colleagues.

Then one summer, while on vacation, I found an isolated spot on the edge of the lake where we were camped, and prayed. But when I was finished, I had the strong sense that I wasn't finished. That God wasn't satisfied. It seemed that the Spirit was saying to me, "Your bundle is too small. We're going to enlarge it. From now on you are going to pray, not just for your family and friends and a few leaders in your congregation. You are going to pray for every member, every contact, everybody that has any connection with that church, by name. And you are going to do it every day."

"But, Lord, you're talking about hundreds of people. I'll never get anything else done!" And the answer that came back was, "This is more important than anything else you will do. Start now. I will help you bring them to mind."

The Lord may be calling you to a different kind of intercession. Perhaps he wants you to pray deeply for a few people that he lays on your heart. If you already have a "bundle" of people you pray for daily, trust the Spirit to enlarge it or reduce it as he pleases.

If you haven't been in the practice of interceding, start with your family, your pastor, your friends, the people who live near to you, the boss at work. If you commit yourself to the practice of intercession, you will receive help from the Spirit of God. Remember, it's not your program, it's the Spirit's, and he knows how and where you will fit. And he will empower your prayers to accomplish everything they are meant to.

But let's be practical, you may be thinking. Where am I going to find the time? A mother with three small children has very little time that she can use as she chooses. Most jobs these days are high stress. When the day ends, we're weary and drained. So where does a person with a tight schedule and a long commute find time to get alone (luxury!) and pray?

Once you're convinced that intercession is an essential part of your ministry (remembering that every believer has a ministry, no matter where a paycheck comes from) you turn to the Lord of time and ask for help. "Lord, if this is something you are calling me to do, show me where I am to find the time." He will. He may guide you to establish a beachhead of fifteen minutes a day—early in the morning or late at night, or when little Joshua is down for a nap. Better fifteen minutes every day than an hour off-again, on-again. Once the discipline of fifteen minutes a day has been established, it can be expanded. God will help you.

Be certain of this: God will use your intercessions, more than anything you do, to spread the fire of revival to others. Because this ministry takes place away from human eyes, it is less likely to be done with a divided heart. You are simply putting yourself at God's disposal as you lift these names before the throne. And the Spirit will move through those prayers to accomplish things that can only be accomplished when people pray.

Why God has chosen to tie his redemptive activity on earth to the prayers of his people is beyond our comprehension. But he has. "And will not God vindicate his elect, who cry to him day and night? Will he delay long over them? I tell you, he will vindicate them speedily" (Lk 18:7-8).

There Are No Experts in Prayer

When it comes to prayer, we are all at the same level—all our lives. We are beginners. The men and women who are most disciplined and developed in their prayer life are always the most childlike in their approach to the throne. They know that their prayers are empty without the help of God's Spirit.

Musicians continuously improve their technique. Doctors keep honing their skills. But prayer is different. It is not a skill. Prayer is not a technique. Of course there will be form and order in our prayer lives. We may find it helpful to write some prayers or to read the prayers of David or Daniel. But we need to follow the example of our Lord Jesus and keep them simple.

The minute our prayers become "clever," we are in danger of communing with our egos rather than with the Father. Prayer rises from our hearts with integrity and power only as we remain poor in spirit.

The apostle Paul had been a man of intense prayer for many years when he wrote to the believers in Rome:

> Likewise the Spirit helps us in our weakness; for we do not know how to pray as we ought, but the Spirit himself intercedes for us with sighs too deep for words. And he who searches the hearts of men knows what is the mind of the Spirit, because the Spirit intercedes for the saints according to the will of God.
>
> ROMANS 8:26-27

Paul confessed his utter dependency on the Holy Spirit to help him to pray. He never gave the impression that prayer was something he was "good at." Prayer was simply something he did and that he expected all believers to do.

The only "experts in prayer" are in the Godhead: the Son and the Holy Spirit. It is to them that we keep turning for help throughout our lives.

First, we turn to Jesus' teaching and example. Read whatever books on prayer you find helpful, but remember that the best instructions on prayer you will ever find are in the New Testament Gospels. Jesus left us no directions about how to preach. He just said, "Preach the kingdom." Nor did Jesus give us any guidelines on how to heal. He just said, "Heal the sick, cast out demons." But Jesus gave us a wealth of teachings about prayer:

- "And in praying, do not heap up empty phrases" (Mt 6:7).

- "Pray then like this: Our Father who art in heaven" (Mt 6:9).

- "Whenever you stand praying, forgive, if you have anything against any one" (Mk 11:25).

- And he told them a parable, to the effect that they ought always to pray and not lose heart (Lk 18:1).

- He also told this parable to some who trusted in themselves ... and despised others: "Two men went up into the temple to pray, one a Pharisee and the other a tax collector" (Lk 18:9-10).

- And he said to them, "Why do you sleep? Rise and pray that you may not enter into temptation" (Lk 22:46).

Jesus' teachings were reinforced by the example of his life. Even though the Gospels give us only glimpses of Jesus' prayer life, they show us enough to reveal that prayer was the primary work of his ministry. In the Gospel of Luke we see every major event of Jesus' ministry accompanied by prayer: his baptism, his healing ministry, the choosing of the disciples, his transfiguration, his crucifixion. This record of Jesus' prayer life was preserved for our instruction.

Second, we avail ourselves of the Holy Spirit's ongoing help. We don't know how to pray as we ought, says Paul, a man of prayer. But never mind, he insists, the Spirit of God is there to help us, and even to intercede for us. All we have to do is plunge in and begin to pray with open hearts, and the Spirit will be there to guide us.

Your personal revival is meant to be, above all things, a revival of your prayer life. The Spirit of God comes into your life to lift your prayers into a new dimension, where prayer is no longer your lifeline *to* God, it's your life *with* God. Deep within you, even while you go about the business of daily living, there is a region where prayer ascends and the heart listens. Your discipline of daily time alone with God produces a life that breathes prayer as naturally as your lungs breathe air. Through such a prayer life your will is joined to the will of the Father, and the fire within you begins to spread to others.

Prayer Is the Most Important Thing We Do

If preachers feel that preaching is the most important thing they have to do, their preaching will fall short. If teachers consider teaching their most important work, their teaching will lack authority. Far more important than preaching or teaching or healing or decision making is praying. All our service to God is built on a foundation of prayer.

To acquire bread for the spiritually hungry, we turn to the Father and ask (see Lk 11:5-13). To be able to walk through the chaos of this world without losing our vision of the kingdom, we discipline ourselves daily to ask God to renew our minds in his Spirit (see Rom 12:2). We do not pray so that our work will go well. We pray, knowing that prayer is the work. Prayer is the most important thing we do, because it brings us into communion with God. Prayer brings the atmosphere of heaven into our earthly lives. It is the miracle by which the Word becomes flesh in our daily walk. From the time we rise in the morning until the time we fall asleep at night, there is not an act that we perform that has more impact upon our day, and upon the tomorrows beyond, than prayer.

Prayer Is the Most Difficult Thing We Do

Picture a modern evangelist taking a break from his grueling schedule to visit his aging Aunt Lucy at Sunset Acres. Aunt Lucy is waiting in the chapel for the Wednesday afternoon service to begin.

"The preacher must have forgotten about us," says Lucy to her evangelist nephew. "Could you bring us a few words?"

Graciously, the evangelist opens his Bible and begins to speak to the little flock of elderly residents about prayer. "I know that most of you can't do the things you once could. But you can still pray...."

It seems like an uplifting message to the evangelist. But, as he is about to leave, the evangelist feels a tap on his shoulder. He looks up into the face of a tall resident with a slight smile playing through his thin white beard.

"Just a minute, Sonny, I want to talk to you."

The evangelist isn't used to being called "Sonny." Besides, he is running late and doesn't have time to waste.

The man with the thin white beard holds the evangelist's arm in a surprising grip and, looking down into his harried face, says, "The arena, my friend, is not out there where you preach to tens of thousands. The arena is where you go into your room and shut the door and pray. When you assured us that we 'can still pray' it sounded as if you were telling us that prayer is the easy part. Believe me, Sonny, it's time you should know that prayer is the hard part. Learn that, and you'll see things happen in your ministry you never saw before."

Like the well-meaning evangelist, we sometimes think that prayer belongs especially to the elderly and the infirm. They no longer have strength to engage in the real battles of life, so they pray for us while we fight in the arena. There are indeed elderly and sickly people who are mighty in prayer, but only because they are much stronger than the world supposes. For nothing we do is more difficult to do well and to do effectively than to pray.

It is no secret that the enemy attacks our prayer life. If he controls our prayer life, he controls us. So distractions visit. A fly bounces against the window. Our minds wander. Fantasies crowd into our thoughts. Doubts challenge: What good is this doing? Is God really listening? To persevere through all this and continue to pray with a mind focused on God is labor.

The freedom and power with which the Father worked through Jesus was a tribute to Jesus' continuous labor in prayer. Observe him praying in Gethsemane. It was work. It was labor so heavy that he asked three disciples to stay awake with him and help carry the weight of it.

When people approach prayer as if it were one of their lighter duties, they will soon be sleeping with Peter, James and John. They misunderstand what is involved. And they will be distracted or bored or lulled to sleep or demoralized by the enemy of prayer. Far better to come to prayer with the knowledge that this is going to be work. It is in fact the most difficult work we have ever begun. To pray well and to pray consistently, day after day, will require more perseverance than we have ever applied to anything in our lives.

Prayer Is the Most Effective Thing We Do

Before Jesus sent his disciples out into the harvest, he commanded them to pray. "Pray therefore the Lord of the harvest to send out laborers into his harvest" (Mt 9:38). That is, first connect with God's will (through prayer), then move into whatever action is called for.

We would do well to save the breath we spend talking to a person who does not want to listen to us and convert our talk to prayer. The only access we have to that closed ear, that bitter heart, is through the Lord who hears our prayer. Pray for that person, in love, laying aside all resentment, and God himself will prepare the way.

When Jesus promises us that if we ask anything of the Father in his name, he will do it, we often thank him for the offer and refuse to take it seriously. We find it so hard to receive this promise with childlike confidence and start asking. So he waits. But when we repent of our proud unbelief, become children and draw near to the Father, asking in the name, the mind, the will, the nature of Jesus, things begin to happen. Always. The most effective thing we can do is pray.

Prayer Is the Most Lasting Thing We Do

What became of the prayer I prayed this morning? When the carpenter drives in a nail, it stays. When the mason builds a wall, it stands. But these words I uttered alone before God, this morning, seem to have left not a trace behind them.

The truth is that those fragile words of prayer have already left a mark on the universe that will remain long after the carpenter's nail and the mason's wall have ceased to exist.

I do not pray for these only, but also for those who believe in me through their word, that they may all be one; even as thou, Father, art in me, and I in thee, that they also may be in us, so that the world may believe that thou hast sent me.

JOHN 17:20-21

The effects of this prayer of Jesus continue to this moment. Nations have come and gone. Entire civilizations have disappeared since this prayer was prayed in the Upper Room, and the answer to this prayer continues to unfold. Long after heaven and earth, as we know them, have passed away, the answer to this prayer will shine with splendor as the Bride of Christ walks with her Bridegroom without spot or wrinkle.

The labor of prayer becomes easier when we remember that it is worth the effort. Not a word is wasted. The Father who hears our prayer lifts and holds our heart-cries in the eternal realm. If the evil that we bind on earth is bound in heaven, it is bound forever. If the captives that we free on earth are freed by heaven, their chains are broken for eternity.

> And this is the confidence which we have in him, that if we ask anything according to his will he hears us. And if we know that he hears us in whatever we ask, we know that we have obtained the requests made of him. If any one sees his brother committing what is not a mortal sin, he will ask, and God will give him life for those whose sin is not mortal.
>
> 1 JOHN 5:14-16

Death and decay cannot undermine the work that is accomplished as a result of our intercessions. The beauty of the Lord our God has come to rest upon us, and the work of our hands is established beyond all time in answer to our prayers.

NINE

Revival in Worship

Then I looked, and I heard around the throne and the living creatures and the elders the voice of many angels, numbering myriads of myriads and thousands of thousands, saying with a loud voice, "Worthy is the Lamb who was slain, to receive power and wealth and wisdom and might and honor and glory and blessing!" And I heard every creature in heaven and on earth and under the earth and in the sea, and all therein, saying, "To him who sits upon the throne and to the Lamb be blessing and honor and glory and might for ever and ever!" And the four living creatures said, "Amen!" and the elders fell down and worshiped.

REVELATION 5:11-14

Revival takes place wherever the atmosphere of heaven touches the earth. Jacob was revived in his night vision-dream, when he saw angels ascending and descending upon a ladder to heaven. The disciples were revived when they saw Jesus alive from the dead. And in each case, the human heart responded with worship. "And when they saw him they worshiped him" (Mt 28:17).

Worship: the human heart responding to glory which has come near, offering itself to God in thanksgiving, spending itself in praise. Worship cannot be engineered. No one can manipulate another person into a state of worship. Church leaders can turn down the lights, play soft music and invite us to close our eyes or raise our hands. But it only becomes worship when we choose of our own free will to present our bodies to God as a living sacrifice, when we choose to lift our hearts to God in thanksgiving and praise.

Nobody had to teach the Samaritan leper how to worship. He stood for a moment and looked at his arms. His skin was clear for the first time in years! Who but God could do a thing like this? Something inside the man's heart broke loose. His mouth opened, and out flowed a river of praise. Lord God, I adore you! I give you praise! Hallelujah!

The Samaritan turned, ran back to where Jesus was standing and threw himself at Jesus' feet. Thank you, Master! Thank you! Thank you!

It is significant that Jesus never prescribed the "proper" way to worship. It didn't seem to matter to him whether the hands were up or down, whether the eyes were open or shut. The Samaritan leper shouted. That was fine. The woman who washed Jesus' feet with her tears and wiped them with her hair never spoke a word. That was fine. Mary anointed Jesus' feet with expensive ointment, worth a year's wages. That was fine. Any expression of thanksgiving was fine with Jesus. It doesn't seem to matter to God *how* we worship. But it matters a great deal to God *that* we worship, that we express to him the thankfulness of our hearts in Spirit and in truth. "For such the Father seeks to worship him" (Jn 4:23).

Yet many of us seem to have trouble expressing our appreciation to God. Personal revival ignites our hearts, and we want to worship. But we are at a loss.

We're like the young man who longs to be able to tell the woman sitting across from him at the table how much he loves her. The sun is setting over the ocean. The birds are singing. The man's heart is full. His beloved sits there, waiting for him to say what she knows is in his heart.

He blurts out, "What time is it?"

He needs to say, "I love you." He wants to say, "I love you." And all he can produce is, "What time is it?"

Something seems to inhibit our worship. Even in Pentecostal churches and charismatic fellowships, where more expressive worship is encouraged, the freedom of praise time often has difficulty following believers into their daily lives. They desire to keep on praising God as they drive the bus or mop the kitchen floor, but their fervor dissipates as the worries of the day crowd in.

Just as the Evil One strives to undermine our prayer life, he will also do whatever he can to stifle our worship of God, either by inhibiting it or by inflating it into an emotional balloon that has no substance. The enemy attacks our worship, because he knows worship is an essential part of our life with God. It is not too strong to say that if the revived heart cannot worship God, it will die. It must find a way to express its thanksgiving to God. It must find a path of expression for its praises.

Private Worship

As we experience personal revival, the Holy Spirit begins to help us to express our praises, first in our private, personal worship life. He helps us, but we have to open up and let those praises flow.

Don't bottle them up. Don't quench them. Your heart wants to say, "Father, I love you! Jesus, I love you!" It wants to give thanks. It wants to offer praise to God. But you have to open your mouth and give it permission to speak.

Don't just think it. Say it. Or sing it. If there are other people in the house, and you're not comfortable having them hear your private worship, shut the door of the room and whisper. But begin to speak your thanksgiving.

Jesus himself is our example in this. We have only brief glimpses of Jesus' inner life, but we see enough to behold a Son who adored his Father and *expressed* his adoration: "I thank thee, Father, Lord of heaven and earth, that thou hast hidden these things from the wise and understanding and revealed them to babes; yea, Father, for such was thy gracious will" (Mt 11:25-26). And, "Now is my soul troubled. And what shall I say? 'Father, save me from this hour'? No, for this purpose I have come to this hour. Father, glorify thy name" (Jn 12:27-28).

Every time Jesus held a loaf of bread in his hands, he lifted his eyes to heaven and gave thanks. His daily life breathed with an atmosphere of adoration for his Father. He wasn't ashamed to speak of his Father anywhere or at any time. "My Father ... my Father" was constantly on his lips, because that's where his heart was.

When you are alone with God, feel free to fall on your knees or to lift up your hands. The more you learn to worship God in your private time with him, the easier it becomes to translate that worship into a life lived among people. Alone with God you present your body as a living sacrifice. Out among people, on your job, in the neighborhood and in your church, your physical body continues to worship God as it washes dishes, repairs cars, teaches school, does word processing, prescribes medication, sells clothing. Deep within there is a temple where thanksgiving constantly rises as incense to the Father, whose Spirit has ignited you, and to the Son who is guiding your steps.

Corporate Worship

The Samaritan leper who has been healed begins his new life worshiping God with all his heart. But he is alone and needs to have fellowship. Somehow, in the providence of God, this man will be directed into the company of others who have seen the glory. They too love God. They too are thankful to Jesus for his unspeakable mercy.

But what if these people express their worship to God in a different way? Should the Samaritan keep looking until he "finds the right church"? Maybe. Maybe not.

The Lord we worship in our inmost hearts leads us into the company of others who love him and, by his Spirit, he teaches us to join them in worship—even if their way of expressing their praise differs from ours.

We are tempted to run ahead of the Holy Spirit and prescribe for others a kind of worship which is more our choice than God's. The form of worship (or lack of form) is not what causes it to burn with God's life. The cloud of God's glory can descend upon any kind of worship. What makes worship live is the attitude of our hearts. Do we bring with us into the assembly an attitude of praise?

Have you ever heard a complaint like this?

On Friday evening I went to a praise meeting where there must have been a thousand people gathered to worship God. It was a foretaste of heaven! Hearts were uplifted, hands were raised, as the singing carried us out of ourselves into the presence of the Lord. Then there was a hush, as everyone waited for the Spirit to lead. One had the feeling that the whole assembly had laid its cares at the feet of Jesus and had become children in his presence. God inhabited the praises of his people that evening. Toward the end of the meeting a word came forth. It was clear, powerful and sent us on our way charged with fresh life. My spirit was renewed.

But Sunday morning, when I went to my church, the contrast was painful. The service was stiff, weighed down with centuries of tradition. The choir offered a good anthem. Our pastor brought a helpful message. But compared with Friday evening, could you call this worship?

Many of us have not only heard such complaints, we have raised them ourselves. What do we do when our church's worship is earthbound and dull? ("Let us now sing hymn 347...." "We will read responsively Psalm 46 on page 241...." "Don't forget to support the bake sale this Saturday.") Or what do we do when the worship team seems to be turning worship into a performance? Or when two or three personalities seem to dominate the flow of the praise time?

We are told that Jesus went to the synagogue on the Sabbath "as was his custom." Jesus was a practicing Jew. As a practicing Jew he adhered to the Jewish liturgies he had known all his life. Doubtless, there were synagogues where there was fervor, and there were synagogues where the worship was dry as dust. But Jesus was always there, praying the ancient prayers, responding to the cantor with hymns and chants he had known from the days of his childhood. Jesus wasn't merely going through motions. He was worshiping Adonai, his Father, in the midst of the great congregation of Israel! If the cantor was off key, or if the lector stumbled over a word, or if the man next to him fell asleep, it was no less worship. Jesus didn't depend for his "lift" on the atmosphere around him. He brought an atmosphere of worship with him.

Can you picture Jesus coming away from the synagogue and complaining, "That place is dead! Those people don't know how to worship; they're keeping the lid on too tight!" Never. Nor could you imagine Jesus complaining, "That synagogue is out of hand! Those people are getting a little too happy. Somebody needs to bring things under control!" Jesus had plenty to say about hypocrisy and hardness of heart, when he was confronted by the scribes and Pharisees. But we never hear Jesus critiquing their worship. He joined himself to it. He stood in their midst and worshiped as one of them.

Your worship in the congregation—any congregation—is not dependent on the atmosphere around you, *but on the atmosphere you bring to it.* Come to that assembly with a broken spirit and a contrite heart, and your worship will be ignited. Your own attitude either welcomes the Spirit or grieves him. If you welcome the Spirit, if your heart gives praise to the Lamb that was slain, the atmosphere around you will be enriched.

The common belief is that vital worship is only possible when the atmosphere is right. No one can deny that, when the hearts around us are uplifted in praise, it is easier for us to praise God. But suppose the atmosphere around us is cold. Does this make it impossible for us to worship? Not at all. If our Lord could worship in any synagogue, by his grace, we can worship in any church. And our worship will contribute, rather than detract, as we join our hearts in love to the people around us.

But suppose you see a way in which your congregation's worship can be improved. You feel it would be helpful if the worship team introduced an occasional time of silence after a chorus, to allow people to reflect on the words they just sang or to pray. Approach the people on the worship team and share your thoughts. If they receive your suggestion and include it in the next praise gathering, fine. If they have reservations about this change, leave it with them and with the Lord.

Shortly after revival broke out at Messiah Church and our Wednesday evening Bible study mushroomed from fifteen people to one hundred fifty, as a "bold departure" we decided to open the meeting with a song. After several months of this one-song opening (followed by prayer), Dave Yon came up to me and said, "Couldn't we have a little more than one song to open this Bible study? We like to sing. We want to worship a little." Dave had put his finger on what we lacked. The one-song opening gave way to a time of worship led by a group of musicians and singers who helped us all to leave the cares of the day behind us and lift our hearts in praise to God.

Or suppose you are the worship leader or on the worship team. This puts you in a place of responsibility under God for doing everything you can to help encourage genuine worship. While worship cannot be engineered, it can certainly be aided or hindered by the people who lead it. You are called and gifted to lead these people into the presence of God, to help them "take off their shoes" as they stand on holy ground, to encourage them to believe that Jesus is once again keeping his promise to come into the midst of disciples who have gathered in his name. So you prepare for worship by having everything ready that can be made ready. The team knows and is in agreement about what it is going to do. The worship leaders pray. And then you take your place before the assembly, fully conscious that you stand before these people in the name of the Lord Jesus himself. You are going to help them find their way into his presence as they lift their hearts in praise.

Whether we are leading or participating, it is important to make sure that five essential elements of corporate worship are present every time we gather to give thanks to God. They are: (1) waiting for the Lord; (2) praise and thanksgiving; (3) reconciled hearts; (4) unity; (5) continuity.

Waiting for the Lord

"I wait for the Lord, my soul doth wait, and in his word do I hope. My soul waiteth for the Lord more than they that watch for the morning" (Ps 130:5-6, KJV). In all worship there is the element of waiting. We are waiting for the Lord to come to us, to manifest himself in some way, to speak. We await his pleasure, not he ours.

He promised that he would never leave us desolate. He would come to us. So we begin with that promise and wait for him, as we stand in the congregation and worship. We are not waiting for a feeling to come over us. We are not waiting for bells to ring. We are waiting for the Lord himself.

And we are not waiting alone. We are surrounded by brothers and sisters who love him as we do, and we are joined to them as we wait. We see their faces and thank God for the privilege of worshiping with these people. Some of them have been faithful to the Master at great cost to themselves. Some of them have experienced suffering such as we have never known. There are men and women in this congregation whose hearts are overflowing with gratitude. Others are here because they are looking for some sign of hope. But all of them are waiting, like Elijah standing at the mouth of the cave, waiting for God to make himself known.

Lord, I want to open my spirit wide to you. I want to meet you in the voice of a gentle stillness. I want to praise you "in the great congregation." I want to join my heart to my sisters and brothers as you join your heart to them, so that nothing will hinder our praises.

Praise and Thanksgiving

One Wednesday night during worship I looked over toward the window and saw John with his hands raised toward heaven in praise to God. His were the only hands that were raised at that moment. But this was not merely John with his hands up. I was looking at praise incarnate. This man was offering himself back to God for the miracle of a transformed life. He did not need the support of a thousand other uplifted hands to give him the courage to express his praise.

Nor was John trying to "set an example." He was just giving thanks to the Lord Jesus who had lifted him out of the shadows and brought him into the light. Praise is the expression of a grateful heart, but it begins with an act of the will.

"I *will* bless the Lord at all times: his praise *shall* continually be in my mouth. My soul *shall* make her boast in the Lord: the humble shall hear thereof, and be glad" (Ps 34:1-2, KJV, emphasis added).

You choose to express to God the thanks you feel in your heart. Now the words of that hymn or chorus you are singing with the others take wings and fly toward the throne. Your faith is strengthened as you express the gratitude that was cramped and bottled within you. Somehow the assembly is helped in its praises by your praises.

But suppose the atmosphere of praise seems to be missing. A heaviness hangs over the gathering. Isn't it harder to give praise and thanks to God when there's no life in the place? It may be harder, but not impossible. Our Lord continued to give thanks to his Father, even when he was surrounded by skeptics (Mt 11:24-25). If you decide before God that you will "bless the Lord at all times," that his praise shall continually be in your mouth, the Spirit will help you express your praise and thanksgiving to God even when the service is restrained and the music drags.

Reconciled Hearts

Whatever we offer to God is an act of worship—our praises, our bodies as living sacrifices, our gifts of money, our fasting, our hymns of thanksgiving. Worship is offering ourselves back to God in thanksgiving. When a gathering of believers offers itself to God in worship, heaven touches earth and the very walls around us tremble at the presence of the One who draws near and fills our house with his glory.

But suppose, as I look across the room, I see a man who is angry with me. Yes, I know why he is angry. It's over something unbelievably petty. So let him simmer. If he chooses to walk around in a snit over the fact that I forgot to mention his name as one of the landscapers who put in those five bushes near the church entrance, that's his problem. There he is, singing, "This is the day that the Lord has made." But when our worship ends, he will avoid me. And here I am, singing the same words, trying to keep my mind on things above; but I'm distracted by his attitude.

"So if you are offering your gift at the altar, and there remember that your brother has something against you, leave your gift there before the altar and go; first be reconciled to your brother, and then come and offer your gift" (Mt 5:23-24). Jesus commands us to interrupt our worship as soon as we remember that this person has something against us.

Drop everything. Leave your gift there before the altar, and go. Because your worship will not rise beyond the ceiling until you have made a genuine attempt to get things right with that brother.

It's not just "his problem." It's yours as well. How can the

Spirit of God ignite your worship or his, when the dark fires of resentment pollute your relationship?

I will have more to say about reconciliation in chapter eleven, but it is important, in this discussion of revived worship, to understand that worship and reconciliation can never be separated.

The best gift you can offer to the worship of that assembly is to slide over to the man during the next chorus, and say, "Can we talk?" Go for coffee. Whisper in the vestibule. Do whatever you have to do to be able to say to this person privately, "Will you forgive me? I want to make things right between us. I will do whatever is necessary to restore our friendship." When you return to the assembly, your worship, and the worship of that church, will be enhanced by your obedience to the Word.

Unity

Sometimes in our frustration with lifeless worship we try to help it along, to "prime the pump."

I remember a "prophecy" which came from a sister who felt that she had been patient long enough. "My children, lift your hands and worship me! If you keep resisting my call to raise your hands in worship, I shall have to leave this place." The woman had made a few sacrifices to join herself to this rag-tag fellowship and was convinced that the Lord had put her there to help it to rise out of its inhibitions into a full-blown "charismatic format."

The elders had to decide whether the prophecy was coming

from the Holy Spirit or from this dear sister who wanted only the best for the church. They decided that the prophecy came from the woman's well-meaning spirit rather than the Holy Spirit, and the worship of that assembly continued to follow its own unique course, which somehow attracted charismatic Christians, anti-charismatic Christians and everything in between.

For our unity in worship is not the *way* we worship, but the *One* we worship: Jesus. We are gathered in his name, covered by his blood, submitted to his Spirit. We partake of one loaf, drink of one cup.

The best contribution I can make to unity in worship is to approach the men and women who worship with me in an attitude of unpretentious friendship. I have far more to learn from them than they from me. I draw near to them, not as a superior, but as a peer, with the simple desire to join my heart to theirs, and theirs to mine, in worship. "O magnify the Lord with me, and let us exalt his name together" (Ps 34:3, KJV). Magnify him any way you choose. Praise him in whatever way seems best to you, and I'll join my heart to yours, as we exalt his name together.

Continuity

Revived worship always manifests continuity between the praises expressed in the gathered assembly and the lives that are lived beyond the church walls. We continue to praise God with our service to him in our daily walk. If the life I live with my wife and children does not match my praises in church, my praises are empty. True praise to God becomes a river of living water flowing out of me into the lives I touch. At work. In the neighborhood. On the freeway. In the supermarket. Worship in the assembly has renewed in me a spirit of servanthood. And now I live that servanthood with a heart which never ceases to give thanks to the Father.

> As you come to the city, you will meet a band of prophets coming down from the high place with harp, tambourine, flute, and lyre before them, prophesying. Then the spirit of the Lord will come mightily upon you, and you shall prophesy with them and be turned into another man.
>
> 1 SAMUEL 10:5-6

Samuel promised Saul that, as he worshiped, he would be "turned into another man." He would be empowered to serve God in ways which were impossible to him before. And it happened.

So our worship in the gathered assembly empowers us to serve God in Spirit and in truth—in everything we do. We gather in the name of Jesus to worship the Father; the Spirit comes upon us afresh as we lift our hearts in praise; and we are turned into "another man," "another woman." Then we go forth into a troubled world—still worshiping God—to manifest the love of Jesus.

TEN

Revival Spreads Through Simple Acts of Service

Once your heart has ignited through personal revival, you become a torch in God's hand. Wherever God brings this torch into contact with other lives, the fire is able to spread to them. The Spirit's redemptive life in you flows out as you come into contact with other people.

But the contact has to be genuine. Your heart has to be open to them, even as it is open to the Lord. As the Pharisees passed through the marketplace, they brushed against all kinds of people. Yet it was as if the Pharisees were far above the ordinary citizens of Jerusalem, the tax collectors and sinners. They were aloof, insulated by their "righteousness," so that there was no personal flow between the Pharisees and ordinary people who surrounded them as they passed through the city.

Jesus, on the other hand, moved among people as one who was available. He ate with tax collectors and sinners. He lived among them as their servant. "For which is the greater, one who sits at table, or one who serves? Is it not one who sits at table? But I am among you as one who serves" (Lk 22:27). And Jesus taught his disciples to follow his example. To serve people we have to come near to them and allow them to come near to us.

During the first few years we lived in Detroit, our family was housed in a church-owned parsonage in a quiet neighborhood, far from the church. It was a safer place to live than the church neighborhood. The schools were better. But the people who lived in the shadow of our church would often ask, "Where do you live?"

I knew what they meant by that question. Are you one of us, or are you above us? You're not afraid to come here to preach. Are you afraid to come here to live?

My wife Jean and I talked about it and prayed about it. Lord, you gave us four children. If you want us to serve Messiah Church, we believe you also want us to live in the church neighborhood. We're going to have to trust you to watch over our children in that neighborhood and in those schools.

We scratched together a down payment, with the help of some friends and relatives, and bought a house a few blocks from the church. That "tough" neighborhood received us with more kindness and friendship than any place we had ever lived. Our children probably learned more about the real world in those schools than in all their years of university that followed. And for twenty-three years we lived among people who taught us and gave us far more than we could ever give them.

The fire in our hearts does not leap to others from a distance, by "remote control." It spreads through proximity, simply by being near to others. We need to remove the insulation from our lives and be available to people, so that the fire in us can find its way into their hearts—just by being near them. And the simplest way to be near to people is to "wash their feet," to serve them. Don't worry about giving them the seven steps to salvation or the four spiritual laws. Don't premeditate what you're going to say. Just be there as a servant, in the name of the Lord. Because revival spreads through simple acts of service. "Go preach the gospel," said St. Francis, "if necessary, use words."

Since Jesus commanded us to wash one another's feet, we begin our acts of service in the church where God has placed us. Then we move out beyond the church to the numberless people we encounter in our daily lives who have never tasted the redemptive power of God. And all the while we remember that God is using us as a torch in his hand to ignite the hearts we touch as we serve in simple ways, such as....

Who Needs a Ride?

Not everyone who comes to church owns a car. There are those who would like to be part of a church, if they could only find a way to get there. Some communities do an excellent job of transportation networking. But even in the best of them, people are slipping through the cracks because the bus doesn't run on Sunday or the church building is out in the "boonies."

If we have no car ourselves, we may still be able, with a little chutzpah, to facilitate rides for others. If we own a car it's easy to find people who would appreciate a ride.

Remember, when you are giving someone a ride, you are doing more than giving them a ride; you are touching them in a personal way with the flame of the Spirit that burns in your heart. Don't underestimate what God can do through you, just by your presence with people, as you travel together. Opportunities will come to offer a word of encouragement, a listening ear—opportunities that would never arise if you weren't taking the trouble to provide rides for people.

Help in the Nursery

A few churches have a trained nursery staff. Some hire child-care workers. But for most churches, the nursery is a volunteer proposition and is often needy and shorthanded. Young mothers and fathers take their turn, but there's a place for men and women of any age to come and help. Because it is a low-profile job with few rewards to the ego, it's Christian foot-washing at its best. Service. And fellowship too, because there's almost always somebody there besides yourself, helping to watch over and care for these little ambassadors of the kingdom.

But how can a person spread revival in a nursery? That's what the disciples thought, and they tried to brush the mothers away. But Jesus rebuked them. He had time for the little ones and their mothers, because they were very important to him. They still are.

Visit a Shut-In

Synneuve is close to ninety. Her husband, Sig, died a few years ago, and she lives by herself in a little house on the north end of town, surrounded by neighbors who are like sons and daughters to her. Synneuve loves company. Her face lights up when she welcomes you. "Cup coffee?" she asks in her rich Norwegian accent. But no one from church has been to see her for a month. She needs a visit from one of us.

Don't worry about conversation. She'll keep it going. A few questions, and she'll tell you about her life, of her years of separation from Sig during the war, and of beginning again in a new land. She loves to talk about her son, Svein, and his family, who live in another city. And she'll finish off by telling you how good God is.

So call a friend and say, "Let's go see Synneuve." Drink her coffee and listen to her wisdom. She'll be pleased if you offer to pray for her.

Are you bringing revival to Synneuve's house? Of course. But more important, the Spirit of the Lord will quicken the revival in you as you visit her. She will teach you, if your heart is open to it, how important it is to be there for another person, how powerfully God uses a listening ear.

Open Your Life to a Local Survivor

John called just to ask how you're doing. In passing he mentioned that he's down to ten cigarettes, two cans of soup, a loaf of bread and a little coffee. He didn't ask for anything, mind you, but he'd be delighted if someone would come through with some groceries or a few dollars.

John isn't what you'd call an "active church member." He lives by himself in a small apartment on an even smaller disability check. Through you, he's part of the church. He's a sheep who needs to be fed in more ways than one. Go see him, and if you could spare a few dollars, John would be grateful.

You may not see the flame of revival leap across the kitchen table and ignite John's heart, but you will know the Spirit of God has moved you to be there. You will be aware that whatever material help you give this man is conveying a sacramental blessing, a heavenly gift flowing through something as earthly as a can of soup or a loaf of bread. Any revival that doesn't quickly flow out and touch people like John with material help will be short-lived.

Join a Small Group—or Start One

One of the best places to discover opportunities to serve is in one of the small groups in your church. In the Sunday morning adult class, the Wednesday-night Bible study, one of the cell groups, you will find people who aren't afraid to tell you about an approaching operation, or the depression they're trying to beat or how uncertain their employment prospects are. A small group within the church is where you have a chance to get close to people and let them get close to you.

In such intimate settings the first Christians prayed and worshiped and cared for each other. "And day by day, attending the temple together and breaking bread in their homes, they partook of food with glad and generous hearts, praising God and having favor with all the people" (Acts 2:46-47). On Sunday everybody gets together to celebrate the feast of victory at Jesus' cross and to give thanks for his resurrection. But sometime through the week we need to be with other believers in a smaller setting, where we can share our burdens and our blessings and encourage each other to walk the walk.

If there is no small group meeting in your church, it may be time to start one. Go through whatever channels necessary to have the full approval of the pastor and the leadership. Make sure that the group is open to everybody. Let the gathering start on time and end on time. The meetings need to be warm, friendly, informal, so that every newcomer feels at home. At the same time there needs to be enough structure so that the meeting doesn't sag into idle chatter.

"How's it been going in your life this week?"

"Before we go to prayer, what are the needs, and what are the things to give thanks for?"

"Tonight we're looking at First John, chapter one."

It's great to begin the meeting with some singing and perhaps close with a song. Refreshments should be simple. Having refreshments at the beginning, as people come in, is a good way to encourage fellowship. Then, after closing prayer, people can be on their way with their souls refreshed.

Gathering a small group in a church where there is none is a practical and helpful act of service to its people. An announcement should be made to the whole church, explaining the purpose of this group and making clear that everybody is welcome. But this announcement needs to be followed up with personal invitations. If only three people come on the first evening, don't be discouraged. Three people is a wonderful start. Share your vision of how helpful a small-group setting could be to many in the congregation, and enlist their help. Trust that the Spirit of the Lord will guide you and empower you in this service to his people.

Most Christian bookstores carry books about forming and nurturing small groups. These books can be helpful, as long as you remember that God may have plans for your group that differ in some ways from the models which these books provide.

Help Out on Work Day

Almost every church has a work day, when folks join together to do some special housecleaning. They wash down the chairs, scrub the nursery, plant shrubs, clean windows, sweep the parking lot, paint, do minor repairs. Work day might not seem to be a particularly "spiritual" occasion. Yet it gives you a chance to work side by side with people you've been praying for, people you rarely see except in church on Sunday morning. At noon they'll be serving soup and homemade bread, and you can sit down and eat with people you may never have had a meal with before.

Revival in the New Testament was a very down-to-earth thing. It took place in fishing boats and tax offices. The author of revival, Jesus, did not confine his ministry to the synagogue. He was where people were. He moved among them not as some high-ranking religious dignitary, but as their peer. Jesus preferred to set fire to their hearts in the real world rather than in some spiritual hothouse. And to this day, Jesus often gets more done on work day than in the most elaborate and glowing service. Be there; for you're bound to find his Spirit at work among the sweepers and the window washers.

Get Into the Dishpan

Lily had been attending our church for only a few months. Already she was in the kitchen, helping with the dishes, every time there was a coffee hour.

"Lily, you don't have to be washing dishes all the time," someone said to her.

She smiled and answered, "I love it. And besides, it gives me a chance to get to know the folks."

Clearing the tables, washing dishes, stacking chairs. These simple acts of service put us where we need to be—close to our sisters and brothers in the body of Christ. And we can trust that the Lord will deepen our fellowship with the people we work with, spreading encouragement to others as he chooses.

Serving Beyond the Church Walls

When God revives an individual, that person becomes a torch in his hand to bring fresh fire to the body of Christ. And when God revives a church, that church becomes a "city set on a hill," giving light to all around it. The light of that church shines out to the world through the deeds of its people. "Let your light so shine before men, that they may see your good works [simple acts of service] and give glory to your Father who is in heaven" (Mt 5:16).

The simple acts of service you perform within the body of Christ are only a warm-up for your ministry beyond the church walls. Every time you perform an act of service in obedience to Christ (letting your light shine) beyond the walls of your church, you are spreading revival. You are manifesting the kingdom of God in the clearest possible way.

While revival begins with fresh vision and holy joy, it flowers into a life of thanksgiving to God which is expressed in acts of service toward your neighbor, particularly your neighbor who is suffering. "If any one serves me, he must follow me; and where I am, there shall my servant be" (Jn 12:26). You will find Jesus, not only where two or three are gathered in his name, but also where any man or woman or child on this earth is suffering.

Follow Jesus down from the mountain heights of spiritual vision into the valley of suffering. Every time you perform the simplest act of kindness, even as minor as giving a cup of cold water to someone who is thirsty, you are spreading revival. For you are ministering to none other than the Lord Jesus himself. "Truly, I say to you, as you did it to one of the least of these my brethren, you did it to me" (Mt 25:40).

Human suffering is much closer to us than we allow ourselves to believe. We are inclined to think that international relief organizations stand in for us where people suffer from drought, floods, earthquakes and local wars. After all, we can't be there, and some of our tax dollars are paying for all that rice.

Closer to home, government and church agencies represent us as they strive to help the increasing numbers of people who are falling through our "social safety nets." Some of our offerings find their way there. Yet it all seems so distant.

This feeling of distance is heightened by the reports of television journalists who fly into hunger-ravaged countries, show us the wasted bodies of children and their exhausted mothers and fly out again. Tragic, we say, and hope that the food trucks get there in time. What can we do? It's all so far away.

But when we dare to lift our hearts to the Lord and ask him, "Lord, what do you want me to do about all this suffering?" a very simple answer comes back to us: Start where you are and do what you can.

"I was hungry and you gave me food." Certainly, if you became aware of a family in your church where the children were going hungry, you would find a way to help. But now you learn of a family in the neighborhood going to the food bank, because they just can't make it on their income. So you do what you can. You help the food bank. Or you help the family as anonymously as possible. It's part of the revival. It's putting the love of Jesus into action.

You're watching the evening news and once again find yourself looking into the eyes of a malnourished child in some faraway land. But this time, you hear the Spirit of the Lord encouraging you to do something. You can. It is not beyond your power. You can send a check to Care or World Vision or the church agency of your choice. People who haven't even met the Lord yet are digging into their pockets, like Cornelius the centurion, and sending generous help. Surely the revived sons and daughters of God are going to share their abundance with the hungry. It's part of the revival that spreads most purely through simple acts of mercy.

"I was thirsty and you gave me drink." It's a hot summer day. The city workmen repairing a water main in front of your

house are sweltering in the heat. A pitcher of cold water or lemonade and a few paper cups would refresh them. It seems like a trivial thing, but such a simple act of service spreads God's life to others. Pour a few prayers into that pitcher before you take it out, if you like. But be aware that you are touching lives that you would be able to touch in no other way. Or perhaps you're visiting your cousin in the hospital. The man in the next bed has no one to give him a sip of water. "Would you like a drink?" you say. He nods in gratitude and eagerly draws on the straw you put in his mouth.

Broaden the concept of thirst to include people who are thirsty for an encouraging word, a listening ear or even a smile. Give them a drink in the name of the Lord and know that you are refreshing them with the life of God.

Shortly after we moved into a certain neighborhood, Jean smiled and said hello to the older man across the street. She didn't realize that the neighbors had virtually ostracized this man and his wife for reasons unknown to us. A few minutes later the man was at our door with a beautiful rose he had cut from his garden. Pop Dozer was thirsty for a little warmth from a neighbor and was so grateful when somebody finally smiled and said hello.

"I was a stranger and you welcomed me." People across the earth seem to be returning to their tribal roots. Each tribe is pulling its own people closer together, and pity help you if you belong to the wrong tribe. If you're a Tutsi in Hutu country (or vice versa), or a Croat in a Serb village (or vice versa), or a black in white territory (or vice versa) or an Arab on Israeli terrain (or vice versa), you will be looked upon with suspicion.

You may even be in danger. If you have ever been a CFA ("comes from away"), you have no doubt tasted what it feels like to be an outsider.

Our Lord Jesus was an outsider. "He was despised and rejected by men" (Is 53:3), looked upon with suspicion by the authorities in Jerusalem, constantly harassed by the scribes and Pharisees. By virtue of the fact that we are followers of Jesus, we too are outsiders. We are in the world, but no longer of it. And the world is not at all comfortable with our loyalty to the kingdom of God. For all these reasons it should be easy for us to spot a stranger and give him or her a welcome. A simple act of kindness to welcome a stranger carries with it the comfort of heaven.

No matter what circles in which we travel, there will invariably be a person of another "tribe" who is treated as an outsider. The new person at work who recently moved from another part of the country or who speaks with an accent or wears a turban or attends a mosque. Our job, as servants of the Lord Jesus, is to welcome that person, even if no one else does; even if it costs us.

Make that person know that you are glad to have him or her in the company or the neighborhood. Have the newcomer over for a meal. Help him or her get established. This welcome is not a means to an end (that is, to get them into your church); it is an end in itself. No strings attached. An act of simple human kindness toward a stranger in an unfriendly world.

"I was naked and you clothed me." There were plenty of naked, shivering people in Jesus' day. There are more now. And these

ill-clad ones are not confined to Siberia or northern China. They may live down the block from you or just off the freeway you drive every day. It doesn't take weeks of research to find a family that can't afford to buy decent clothes for its children.

As needs arise, the Spirit will show you what to do. You may want to pass along a coat that you are still wearing. Or you may decide to provide some money to buy something new. Or you may purchase three new blankets for the next blanket drive at church. Surely the fire in our hearts is moving us to do what we can to relieve the chill of a shivering body.

"I was sick and you visited me." When our relatives and friends become ill and land in the hospital, most of us are conscientious about visiting. We bring flowers and gifts and words of cheer. But when the illness drags on over months and years, we tend to lose track of these people. Visits decrease. Days, sometimes weeks, go by without a visit or a phone call. Those long, weary, draining illnesses especially need the comfort of regular visits from people who care. They need someone to touch base with them.

We congratulate ourselves that we saw them three times when they were in the hospital, while they wonder why, since they came home, nobody seems to care anymore. They could use touches of revival, visits to lift their spirits. And we need to let God spread some of the joy he has put into us, into them. Keep the visits going. Stay in touch.

Then there is the loner at work, who rarely speaks to anyone. The boss announces that he's in the hospital for exploratory surgery. Everybody signs a card, which the boss stamps and mails. But is anybody going to go and see this man?

Why, I hardly know him. I wouldn't know what to say. He might be uncomfortable having me come to see him in the hospital when we've hardly spoken ten words to each other in the last five years.

Never mind, says the Spirit. Go.

So you go, and discover that you are the only person who has been to see him. The only one. And he weeps with gratitude.

"I was in prison and you came to me." These days it's not easy to get into a prison to visit someone. Unless you're a member of the clergy or a relative, the answer at the front desk may be, "Sorry, I cannot authorize you to visit this person."

My friend, Ray, took matters into his own hands when he went to the county jail to visit his friend, Eddie. "I'm his brother," Ray insisted, and was given a pass. That was before Ray became a Christian and was still in the habit of fast-talking his way through red tape. If you know someone who has landed in prison, you can begin by writing letters. Prisoners love to receive mail. Perhaps the prisoner can put you on his or her list for visits.

But suppose you don't know any prisoners, and you aren't involved in a prison ministry. Never mind, there are "prisons" that are easy to enter, and "prisoners" whom you do know. Nursing homes, even the best of them, are prisons for those who don't want to be there. Even if the resident is too weary or too sick or too old to express appreciation for your visit, that visit means more than you can measure. You become a link between that person and the redemptive power of God.

Some nursing home residents are so delighted to have someone to talk to, their tongues never stop. They talk about the past. They brag about their grandchildren. All you have to do is listen with an open heart. Other residents are listless. Their minds drift. They look out the window and hardly answer as you try to make conversation. Never mind, you are there in the name of the Lord, and you are reaching out in love to one for whom he died.

Never forget that the most effective way to spread the revival that has come to you is through simple acts of service. The Spirit of God flows out of you as redemptive life as you draw near to other people as a servant:

> You are the light of the world. A city set on a hill cannot be hid. Nor do men light a lamp and put it under a bushel, but on a stand, and it gives light to all in the house. Let your light so shine before men, that they may see your good works and give glory to your Father who is in heaven.
>
> MATTHEW 5:14-16

ELEVEN

Revival Restores Broken Relationships

Wherever the Spirit moves with power, he requires absolute obedience in the area of forgiveness. He brings to our minds broken relationships we have tried to forget and reminds us that the time has come to act. When we reconcile, the revival spreads. When we refuse to reconcile, the revival, at least in us, is quenched. In our Lord's parable of the unforgiving servant, he allows no loophole for people who have tasted the mercy of God and refuse to show mercy to others.

> Then his lord summoned him and said to him, "You wicked servant! I forgave you all that debt because you besought me; and should not you have had mercy on your fellow servant, as I had mercy on you?" And in anger his lord delivered him to the jailers, till he should pay all his debt. So also my heavenly Father will do to every one of you, if you do not forgive your brother from your heart.
>
> MATTHEW 18:32-35

Revival has come to us as a gift from God. But there is a condition: our relationship with our fellow Christian has to be right. If there is resentment in my heart toward my sister, my brother, my neighbor, the line between my heart and heaven is blocked. Or if I am aware that my brother has something against me, and I have done nothing to make it right, my line to heaven is blocked. To clear the vertical line to heaven I first have to clear the horizontal line that connects me to my neighbor.

I can still remember when Nellie started coming to our newly built Church of Our Saviour in Dartmouth, Nova Scotia. Nellie and her husband, Bob, her two teenage daughters and her mother would fill a pew faithfully every Sunday. When we began to have Bible studies, Nellie was there, sitting by herself for a half hour of silence, with her head cocked to one side as if she were saying, "Here I am, Lord, tell me something."

One night he told her something. "Get things right with your cousin Peg." Her head wasn't cocked to one side anymore. It was bent down. Nellie wasn't too happy with this inspiration, because she and Peg had not spoken to each other for thirty years. How do you "get things right" when you haven't spoken with your cousin, who lives in the same town, for thirty years? As the war of indecision raged within her, Nellie kept her thoughts to herself. But after she obeyed and found joy in her obedience, Nellie let us in on what had happened.

She was riding the bus downtown, when Peg got on the bus and took a seat toward the front on the opposite side of the aisle. Nellie broke out in a sweat. She felt trapped—by the Lord. *Today's the day. It has to be done.*

Peg got off the bus on Portland Street, near the ferry. Nellie got off behind her and followed her into the bakery.

At Bible study Nellie described what happened. "I walked up to her and said, 'Peg?'"

"Peg looked at me in disbelief. I had spoken to her. After thirty years I had spoken to her! She never was as stubborn as I am.

"'Nellie,' she said as her eyes filled, and gave me a hug. And then we talked—for the first time in thirty years! I told my mother when I got home that I ate some 'humble pie' today. She laughed and said, 'It's about time.'"

Revival not only draws us closer to God, it also brings us closer to each other. The Spirit searches our hearts, and wherever he finds a severed relationship he raises it out of the darkness into his light. He gives us the power to love and forbear, to humble ourselves and ask forgiveness. And then he requires us to act, often giving us a nudge through our circumstances. It is no coincidence that a certain person turns up again after all these months. Our paths cross at the airport. Or he's sitting across the table from us at the potluck supper. She appears in a dream. The revival is now touching a region of our lives which we have tried to bury in darkness. And we know that if the revival in our heart is to continue, this relationship must be restored. Jesus' teaching is crystal clear: our love for God is a sham if our relationships aren't right.

When Your Brother or Sister Has Something Against You

I'll never forget a particular Friday evening. I was sitting in a meeting at Detroit's Western Y, which was conducted by some young men from our church. Suddenly I remembered that my brother had something against me. It was our nine-year-old son, who bore me no hard feelings, but saw very little of me in those early days of the revival. I was busy "doing the Lord's work."

What am I doing here? I said to myself. I don't belong here. I belong with Marty. I got up and left the meeting.

Jean almost cried when I came in the door. She knew why I had come. Who knows? Maybe she was praying for this.

When we know that we have been unkind or unfair to our brother or sister, whether or not that person holds resentment against us, we need to make it right. Many times there is resentment. That person is wounded and angry about something we did or failed to do, while we dismiss the whole issue as pettiness on his or her part.

Give me a break! we say to ourselves and press on with "the Lord's work," treating the matter as closed and forgotten.

But as far as God is concerned, the matter is not closed and forgotten. A relationship has been broken by our hardness of heart, and, as we seek to draw near to God, we begin to feel uncomfortable.

Something's wrong. Then we remember.

It is time to submit to God's judgment in this matter, rather than our own. "Leave your gift there before the altar and go; first be reconciled to your brother, and then come and offer your gift" (Mt 5:24).

This is not something we can mull over and hesitate about for weeks. "Make friends quickly with your accuser," says Jesus (Mt 5:25). We cannot afford to let that relationship fester, because a broken relationship puts us at a distance, not only from our brother, but from God.

When a Christian Wrongs You

"If your brother sins against you, go and tell him his fault, between you and him alone" (Mt 18:15).

As the Spirit of Jesus continues his work of sanctification in us, he teaches us to have tough skin and tender hearts. Wrongs against us begin to roll off us like rainwater. Offenses that once caused us to lose precious hours of sleep begin to melt into forgetfulness as we learn to forbear and as we remember how many similar wrongs against others we have been guilty of. We find it easier now to forgive on the spot and to pray God's fulfilling mercies on the person who slandered us or broke a promise.

But there are wrongs that need to be addressed. We need to go and talk with the person who has wronged us in the same way that we would discuss things with Sears if they sent us a bill for a refrigerator we never bought.

Suppose you're stranded on a lonely road in the middle of winter with a frozen gas line. You're shivering by your car in the late afternoon, when you see what looks like your best friend's car approaching. Help at last! you say to yourself. Your friend passes without so much as a wave.

He saw me! I know he saw me. Why didn't he stop?

A few days later you visit your friend at his mother's funeral, but not a word is mentioned about the incident. The following Sunday in church your friend notices that you seem a bit out of sorts and asks if you're okay.

"I'm OK," you say. "Why shouldn't I be OK?"

As the weeks pass your friendship begins to deteriorate. You become more distant toward your friend. Your friend shrugs his shoulders and backs away.

One day six months later you ask, "Why didn't you stop and help me when I was stranded on the road last winter? I know you saw me. Why didn't you stop?"

"Oh, so that's what it is," replies your friend. "I knew something was wrong, but I couldn't figure it out. Why didn't you tell me what it was? Don't you remember? That was the day my mother died. They called me from the hospital, and I left work in a daze. She died fifteen minutes after I got to her room. Yes, I saw you, but it just didn't register. Of course I should have stopped. I was wrong. Please forgive me."

Sometimes the problem between you and the brother who has wronged you is not solved when you talk. He insists that the car you bought from him was in perfect working order when you drove it out of his driveway. If the transmission dropped three days later, those are the breaks. He still smiles and says, "Praise the Lord!" when he shakes hands with you in church. "But a refund is out of the question." He lives in a $300,000 home. You can't even afford the down payment on a trailer.

In Matthew 18, Jesus lays out some specific steps to take when a brother won't listen to you. These steps are given for the purpose of maintaining unity in the body of Christ. For how can there be unity in the body, when there is a wall between brothers or sisters? If a brother or sister refuses to repent and make right a definite wrong, the body of Christ, for its own spiritual health, must deal with this person justly. Significantly, Jesus concludes this discourse with his strongest-ever teaching about forgiveness. For in the end, the heart of every man or woman of God must be a heart of forgiveness.

When Another Christian Asks Forgiveness

"Take heed to yourselves; if your brother sins, rebuke him, and if he repents, forgive him; and if he sins against you seven times in the day, and turns to you seven times, and says, 'I repent,' you must forgive him" (Lk 17:3-4).

When Jesus insisted on this kind of forgiveness, the apostles cried, "Increase our faith!" There are wrongs that are hard to forgive. Without God's help, who can do it? Yet the life of faith is nothing less than allowing the forgiveness which has been released into this world at Calvary to flow through us. We receive grace that comes to us through the Lamb's blood; and now we live that grace. Mercy flows in; mercy flows out. What better way to describe what revival is all about?

If we're having trouble forgiving a sister or brother, it has less to do with the size of that person's sin against us than the narrowness of our view of Calvary. We are the servants who are forgiven a million-dollar debt, and now we refuse to forgive our fellow servant his or her debt of a hundred?

Our Monday night Bible studies at Messiah Church were rarely as civilized as most church Bible studies. Perhaps for that very reason they attracted men who would not normally find their way into a church. But one Monday night the tension was about to flare into a fist fight. It all began when Frank and Danny got into an argument over whose people had suffered the most: Frank's people, who were black, or Danny's people, who were Native Americans. They pushed back their chairs. Frank was beginning to rise with his fists clenched, when Milton, whose Jewish people had also suffered, closed his Bible, rose from his seat and declared,

"This is not of God!" and headed for the door.

"Yeah, and what you're doing is not of God either," came a voice from the other end of the table. Milton stopped in his tracks, turned, came back to the table and sat down. "Brothers," he said, "I want to ask your forgiveness for my attitude."

Frank and Danny's anger melted into silence, as Milton's repentance convicted us all.

The body of Christ is a school of forgiveness. God puts us together in this assembly of struggling saints to get some practice in the primary exercise of the Christian life: *forgiveness.*

Believers are often baffled by the fact that more pain seems to be inflicted on them by people inside the body than by those outside. How can this be? I'm being let down by Christians. And then they expect me to forgive them?

What choice do we have? The minute I open my heart to receive the mercy of God that flows from Christ's cross, I am committed to allowing that mercy to rule my heart toward my brother—especially the brother who has deeply wronged me and now comes asking my forgiveness. The more my heart is occupied with thanksgiving for the Lamb who has carried my sin into the grave, the easier it becomes for me to forgive my brother from my heart.

When Your Neighbor Needs You

The rich man was careful not to let his eyes meet the eyes of Lazarus. To look into that man's eyes would be to create a relationship. Then he would be obliged to help him. The rich man would pass Lazarus as if he weren't there. The world of Lazarus was a foreign country to the rich man, and he chose to avoid it. Today he passes Lazarus in haste; he's on his way to the temple to worship God. He brings a generous offering, which endears him to the priest—but not to God. The rich man has ignored God, belittled God, cursed God by passing Lazarus with his eyes averted.

The needs that surround us are legion. We cannot possibly meet them all. But to insulate ourselves against these needs by averting our eyes is to wrap ourselves in darkness.

Let your eyes meet the eyes of Lazarus. Don't be afraid. Speak to him. He is not your inferior, he is your equal. Holy blood was shed for him as for you. And if there is something you can do, or give, to help him on his journey, do it without letting your left hand know what your right hand is doing. Wherever the Spirit of the Lord is, there is freedom. And the highest expression of that freedom is generosity. The believer who is generous has found the road to freedom, and the person in need is the gateway to that road.

In chapter thirteen we will take a closer look at the vital connection between Lazarus—the person in need—and revival. In this chapter on restored relationships, it is important to understand that one of the relationships to be restored is our kinship with our neighbor in need, whoever he or she may be. Since revival produces love—love, in deed and in truth—my needy neighbor becomes my brother, my sister. The Samaritan understood (as the priest and the Levite failed to understand) that the wounded Jewish man by the roadside was now his brother. By virtue of his need the wall between Jew and Samaritan was removed and he was free to cross over and pour oil and wine into the man's wounds, to lift him on his beast and carry him to an inn. If revival means anything at all, it means that the Spirit of God has come to enable us to follow the Samaritan's example.

When Your Brother or Sister Stumbles in From a Far Country

Now his elder son was in the field; and as he came and drew near to the house, he heard music and dancing. And he called one of the servants and asked what this meant. And he said to him, "Your brother has come, and your father has killed the fatted calf, because he has received him safe and sound." But he was angry and refused to go in.

LUKE 15:25-28

At 3:00 A.M. the phone rang. It was East Side John, whom I hadn't seen in six months. John had drifted back to drugs. "I've been robbed. I just got home, and they trashed my apartment. My stereo's gone."

So why are you telling me? You made your bed; roll around in it.

"Oh, that's too bad," I said, as if I were sorry for him.

"Maybe the Lord is trying to tell me something," says John.

"Could be," I answered and rolled over and went back to sleep. I can't remember that I even prayed for this brother who was crying out for some encouragement to come back to the Father's house. I was the elder brother, sulking out in the field, while the Father was preparing a welcome for East Side John.

There was music and dancing in heaven while I slept. Because that night John had come home. It was the beginning of a life of powerful service to the King, which continues to this day. John began scouring Skid Row and loading his aging car with men and women who had slid through a thousand cracks and fallen to the bottom. Soon East Side John was preaching at the Catacombs, an end-of-the-road mission blessed by the angels. But why was I so slow to welcome him, when he came stumbling in from a far country?

Perhaps it's the music and dancing that upsets us. These prodigals who come home, after wasting years of their lives, get a lot more attention than we ever got. God seems to treat them with special favor. And here we are. Lo these many years we have served God, and we never disobeyed his commandments (well, not in the extreme), and he never even gave us a little goat that we might celebrate with our friends. But when this son of his (why should I call him brother?) came, who squandered the Father's living with harlots, he kills the fatted calf for him!

Why do these newcomers to the kingdom have such joy? Why do their prayers seem to be answered so quickly? Why do the Scriptures open for them, when they never studied them as we have? Why does their gospel bear so much fruit? It seems as though they are swept forward by the mighty wind of the Spirit, while we sit here becalmed, waiting.

We're waiting in the wrong place. We're brooding outside the Father's house with an attitude that dampens heaven's joy. And heaven is waiting too—for us. Waiting for us to repent of our self-pity and come in and join the celebration. Welcome your brother! Welcome your sister! "It was fitting to make merry and be glad, for this your brother was dead, and is alive; he was lost and is found" (Lk 15:32).

When Your "Brother" Is Your Spouse

"Likewise you husbands, live considerately with your wives, bestowing honor on the woman as the weaker sex, since you are joint heirs of the grace of life, *in order that your prayers may not be hindered*" (1 Pt 3:7, emphasis added).

If revival turns the body of Christ into a school of forgiveness, one of its major learning centers is marriage. There are those who are called and gifted to remain celibate for the kingdom of God. They have their special path to walk, as the Spirit strengthens them in the holy art of forbearance. But for those in the married state, our walk with our spouse is vital to our walk with God. Every blessing that comes to us through revival is translated into living in our relationship with our spouse.

While Jesus claims priority over every love in our lives, he always treats marriage as a holy thing. This man and woman are one flesh. God has joined them together. Surely if God has joined them together, he intends for them to walk in love. If we aren't serious about caring for each other and submitting to each other in love, how can we possibly be serious about loving God?

"Behold, I stand at the door and knock; if any one hears my voice and opens the door, I will come in to him and eat with him, and he with me" (Rv 3:20). This promise applies to our marriages as well as to our individual lives. If we hear his voice and open the door, the Lord will come in and eat with us. He will teach us how to walk together in love. He will transform every day of our marriage into a wedding feast, a feast of joy, which will last as long as we live.

The Lord will teach us by his Spirit that this marriage is *a thing of royalty.* Our mate is to be treated, in all circumstances, with high honor. Never, even in humor, do we demean our mate.

The most precious gift you will ever receive, man, second only to the gift of Jesus himself, is this woman, your wife. She is your queen. Think of her as your queen. Honor her as your queen.

The most precious gift you will ever receive, woman, second only to the gift of Jesus himself, is this man, your husband. He is your king. Honor him as your king.

Jesus teaches us by his Spirit that this marriage is *a school of forgiveness.* Here the mercy of Calvary is translated into flesh and blood, day-in-and-day-out living. Occasions arise that wound us, disappoint us, shock us, baffle us. How can this woman with whom I share my life be so inconsiderate? How can this man be so insensitive to my needs?

Minor disruptions become the last straw. She fried the eggs too hard. Adam's face is a mile long. "Adam, are you all right?" says Eve.

"Yeah, I'm all right."

"Is there something wrong?"

"No! blast it, nothing's wrong!"

Adam forgets to throw his socks in the clothes hamper five days in a row. Eve comes in from the bedroom with her jaw clenched. What kind of slob did I marry?

"What's wrong, Eve?" says Adam.

"Nothing," says Eve, as she sits down and pretends to be reading the paper. But now the Spirit of the Lord encourages Adam and Eve to communicate. To forgive.

Eve can't change the way Adam snores. Adam can't change the way Eve blows her nose. These things they accept in each other with generous forbearance. In big issues and trivial matters they discover that, as they forgive each other and ask for forgiveness, their love grows deeper, richer.

Jesus teaches us that this marriage is *a place of healing*. His presence in our lives flows with healing power between us.

Adam comes home from an impossible day at work. He is discouraged, angry, afraid for his job. Eve puts her arms around him, draws him to herself. They kiss, and ten tons roll off Adam's back. I have you, my love. What more do I need?

There are times when Eve is the wounded one. Her day was a disaster. She feels overwhelmed. Adam makes her a cup of coffee, sits down and listens, shows his appreciation for the wonderful wife God gave him. The dark clouds vanish. Eve is restored.

Jesus teaches us that this marriage is more than an end in itself, it is *a corporate ministry*. God gave us to each other, so that we could serve him together with joy. Occasionally we meet a couple who have been married for many years and are utterly devoted to each other—to the exclusion of the rest of the world. They live for each other and for no one else. Such love is not love, but selfishness in the extreme. Lazarus lies at their wrought-iron gate and never receives a crumb. One day the illusion will end.

When Jesus enters our marriage, he transforms it into a corporate ministry. God gave us to each other so that we can serve him side by side ... raising the children he has given us ... washing feet in the body of Christ where he has placed us ... welcoming the wounded ones he sends to us. As we serve God together, our love grows richer, deeper. And our prayers rise unhindered.

Enemies

"But I say to you, Love your enemies and pray for those who persecute you, so that you may be sons of your Father who is in heaven" (Mt 5:44-45). How do I deal with the person who despises me because of my color? Or the colleague at work who is after my job and will use any means to discredit me? The person who seems driven by a desire to throw trouble into my path?

The Lord warned us that we would have enemies. There will be people who hate us and seek to do us harm. The enemy poses a danger, not only to our safety or our reputation, but to our spirit. Through our enemy, the Prince of Darkness seeks to lure us into the web of vengeance. He tempts us to look upon our enemy in hatred. And as our heart hardens toward "this deceitful man," "this underhanded woman," it begins to lose its capacity for mercy. A veil drops down between the soul and God.

The only protection against this destructive process is to do exactly what the Master commands—*commands:* love him by faith; pray for him. "Pour out your mercy upon this man, O God, flood his life with your richest blessing. Touch his inmost soul with healing grace."

"I've quit praying for my enemies," said my friend Matthew,

"because every time I pray for them, God blesses them. No prayer that I ever pray gets answered more quickly than my prayers for my enemies. It's not fair!" Everybody at the Bible study laughed with a laughter that acknowledged how close to home Matthew's confession had hit. We knew that the next time Matthew's enemies would strike at him, he would pray for them in spite of himself. But we wondered about our own hearts. Were we even trying, as Matthew was, to pray for our enemies?

Why is it that our enemies seem to prosper in so many ways, even when we don't pray for them? Where's the justice?

Scripture tells us that the day is coming when every wrong that was ever done will be paid for, either by the one who did the wrong or by the Lamb's blood. Every wrong will be righted. Every injustice will be fully addressed.

Meanwhile, as men and women who, by the Spirit of God, are already living in the dimension of the coming glory, we need to be careful about our response to the unjust acts of our enemies. We need to make sure that we are not usurping the role of judge, which belongs only to God. Our job is to love our enemies and to pray for those who persecute us, and leave ultimate justice to the God who sees the whole picture and who makes no mistakes.

Our line to heaven was opened when Jesus died and the veil of the temple was torn from top to bottom. Through that torn veil the Spirit of God has come to us and revived us with the life of heaven. But that line to heaven closes whenever our horizontal lines are blocked. Our relationship with God is tied to our relationships with each other. The Spirit has put within us all the power we need to show mercy to each other, as God has shown mercy to us—to heal broken relationships. All we have to do is step out in faith and obey the ancient Law of Liberty: "You shall love the Lord your God with all your heart, and with all your soul, and with all your strength, and with all your mind; and your neighbor as yourself" (Lk 10:27; Dt 6:5).

TWELVE

Free the Captives

On the evening of that day, the first day of the week, the doors being shut where the disciples were, for fear of the Jews, Jesus came and stood among them and said to them, "Peace be with you." When he had said this, he showed them his hands and his side. Then the disciples were glad when they saw the Lord. Jesus said to them again, "Peace be with you. As the Father has sent me, even so I send you."

JOHN 20:19-21

The disciples were glad when they saw the Lord. This encounter with the risen Lord was revival in the purest sense. The disciples were brought back to life by the sight of the Master and the sound of his voice. But before they could relax and revel in the experience, Jesus gave them orders: "As the Father has sent me, even so I send you."

Revival is a work of the Holy Spirit in which our hearts are set free to live consistently in God's redemptive will. And God's redemptive will is revealed in the ministry of Jesus:

The Spirit of the Lord is upon me, because he has anointed me to preach good news to the poor. He has sent me to proclaim release to the captives and recovering of sight to the blind, to set at liberty those who are oppressed, to proclaim the acceptable year of the Lord.

LUKE 4:18-19

Jesus spent his entire ministry fulfilling those words and now his mantle has fallen to us. We have been revived to bring good news to the poor, release to the captives, sight to the blind, liberty to the oppressed and hope to all who languish in despair.

Multitudes out there have never tasted the love of God. We have been empowered to manifest that love. There are men and women in our immediate circle of friends who have no idea how good life could be if they were released from their fears or resentments or whatever other chains sin has wrapped around their hearts. We have been empowered to set them free.

The Power of the Keys

"I will give you the keys of the kingdom of heaven, and whatever you bind on earth shall be bound in heaven, and whatever you loose on earth shall be loosed in heaven" (Mt 16:19). When Jesus gave Peter the keys of the kingdom, he did not say, "Now, Peter, hang on to these keys; they belong to you alone." Nor did Jesus say, "Make sure, Peter, that these keys never fall into the hands of any except the ordained clergy." Nor did he say, "These keys represent apostolic succession." The keys were for Peter and for any man or woman who, like Peter, confessed Jesus as the Messiah.

Evidence that the privilege—and the responsibility—of binding and loosing is given to the body of Christ on earth appears in Matthew, when Jesus, speaking to all his disciples, says:

Truly, I say to you, whatever you bind on earth shall be bound in heaven, and whatever you loose on earth shall be loosed in heaven. Again I say to you, if two of you agree on earth about anything they ask, it will be done for them by my Father in heaven. For where two or three are gathered in my name, there am I in the midst of them.

MATTHEW 18:18-20

I remember watching this power restore life to a man for whom the experts held out little hope. For thirty-one days Don lay in the ICU. The prognosis was bleak. At first it was, "He probably won't make it." Later, "Expect brain damage, if he emerges from the coma." Every time I came to visit Don, his son Len and some friends would be off in a corner of the hospital lobby, praying.

"Don, you're going to rise out of this death to a new life."

Shaking her head in pity, the nurse approached me, "You're wasting your breath. He can't hear you."

One day Don responded by squeezing my hand. A few days later speech returned. His mind was clear. Through all those weeks, Len and his friends kept their vigil in the lobby. They prayed for Don's complete recovery. They were young and bold and, some would say, a little crazy. Were they crazy to hang on to the promise that they could move heaven to break through the crust of this age with a sign of the kingdom?

The keys of the kingdom of heaven give us access to an invisible door that opens on heaven, wherever we happen to be on earth. When we open this door, the powers of heaven respond to us and cause things to happen on earth that can only happen by heaven's command.

I'm not talking about magic. Magic is when a human presumes to take control of something in the supernatural world by "paying his dues" to the kingdom of darkness. I'm talking about something completely different: about the living God giving us the privilege of serving him in the capacity of sons and daughters, in such a way that we become channels through which the power of the cross of Jesus binds the demons and frees the captives.

When we have the keys, we bind the demons, and heaven says, "Yes, they're bound." And the demons can't move. We loose the captives, and heaven says, "Yes, they're loosed." And the captives walk into freedom. *When we have the keys.*

Without the keys, we can rebuke the demons all day long, and they laugh in our face. We can put on a show of loosing the captives. But when the show is over, the captives are still bound.

The men and women who have the power of the keys and use it are marked by the same two characteristics that marked the apostles: (1) they are radically committed to Jesus; (2) they have accepted Calvary as their destiny.

Keys for the Committed

"Now great multitudes accompanied him; and he turned and said to them, 'If any one comes to me and does not hate his own father and mother and wife and children and brothers and sisters, yes, and even his own life, he cannot be my disciple'" (Lk 14:25-26).

It comes down to a very simple question: who or what comes first in our lives? On what center are our hearts fixed?

I remember a man who put those questions to me with burning power. It all began with a strange little radio broadcast.

I don't know if this guy's on the level, I'd say to myself, but when he talks about Jesus, he feeds my soul. I'd turn on the radio to hear Dr. Michaelson each morning at 6:45. The program lasted fifteen minutes.

Between selling maps of Palestine and raising money for the hungry Jewish children in Algeria, Dr. Michaelson would talk about Jesus. And his words about Jesus seemed to burn with holy fire. He would describe his life in Judaism. How Jesus became his Messiah, always against a background of deep love for Israel, his people.

Shortly after we moved to Detroit, it was announced that Dr. Michaelson from California would be speaking Sunday afternoon at a church on the east side. Here was a chance to see the man and check him out.

The crowd was small. Dr. Michaelson was an old man. He spoke from a high stool to ease the pain in his crippled feet. He could not have skimmed anything from the funds he raised for the hungry Jewish children, since his clothes were worn; there was no limo in sight.

Dr. Michaelson needed a ride downtown to his hotel (one of the cheapest in the city). I volunteered, and on the way to the hotel it was like having Saul of Tarsus riding shotgun in the Volkswagen.

"Do you know Jesus? Do you love him?

"You're a preacher … in a mainline church? Why are you wasting your time in a mainline church?"

What Michaelson was saying to me was, "Are you committed to Jesus all the way? Or are you playing church?" It was a question that ate at me for months afterward, because it seemed to me that the Lord himself was speaking to me through this crusty old disciple. And when revival hit our mainline church a few years later, Dr. Michaelson would have been pleased with the change.

Radical commitment to Jesus cannot be measured by the clothes we wear or the car we drive or the kind of church to which we belong. There were those who tried to measure Jesus' commitment to the kingdom against that of John the Baptist. John wore camel's hair and lived on locusts. Jesus wore a seamless robe and ate with tax collectors. Yet Jesus' commitment to the Father's will was total.

He requires of those who follow him a commitment so strong that, by comparison, every other human love becomes hatred. If we say, "Jesus is Lord," the proof that we mean what we say is that he is Lord over *us*—Lord over every part of our lives.

The growth of Peter's commitment is a pattern that is repeated in our lives. When Peter left his fishing to follow Jesus, he didn't know what he was getting into. Of course, he was honored to be called by the Master. But letting go of his old life was not that easy. Peter loved fishing. Fishing was his life. As he followed Jesus along the shore of Galilee, Peter would see old friends busy with their nets, and he would have to swallow the lump in his throat.

After the resurrection, for old time's sake, Peter decided to take a dip into the past, have a little taste of the life he once knew.

"I'm going fishing," he said to his friends.

"We'll go with you," they answered.

That night they caught nothing.

"Children, have you any fish?" came a voice on the shore, as dawn was breaking.

"No," they answered from the boat.

"Cast the net on the right side of the boat."

Suddenly, fish everywhere! So many fish in the net, it was impossible to haul it up. What more does Peter need to remind him of his call?

Jesus welcomes the disciples to breakfast.

After breakfast: "Simon, son of John, do you love me more than these [fish]?"

"Yes, Lord, you know that I love you."

"Feed my lambs." Where is your commitment, Peter? If it's with me, it cannot be divided. I cannot use you in the service of the kingdom unless you are with me all the way.

The Lord puts the same question to every person who has tasted the renewing power of revival. Do you love me *more than*—whatever else you love? Do I come first in your life, ahead of wife, husband, child, profession, wealth, name? Until revival ignites us, we are inclined to settle for a two-tiered kingdom. On the lower level are those who "believe in Jesus for salvation." They are satisfied to attend church and accept the doctrines. But they are not ready to give up their "fishing." They love Jesus, but not enough to make radical changes in their lifestyles.

"I may not come in for big rewards," they say, "but I'm saved, and that's what counts."

On the upper level are the gung-ho types. They're obsessed

with Jesus; fanatics at prayer. They even give Jesus control of their finances.

"God bless 'em, they deserve the keys of the kingdom, but that's not my cup of tea," say the lower-level saints.

But revival opens our eyes to see that the kingdom of God is not two-tiered. To be born again of the Spirit is to be led by the Spirit into radical commitment to Jesus.

"Do you love me more than these fish?"

"Yes, Lord, you know that I love you."

"Then feed my sheep. And to help you in your work, I give you the keys of the kingdom of heaven. Whatever you bind on earth shall be bound in heaven, and whatever you loose on earth shall be loosed in heaven."

Keys for the Calvary Road

"Whoever does not bear his own cross and come after me, cannot be my disciple" (Lk 14:27). Does bearing a cross mean martyrdom? Perhaps. Peter understood that that's what it meant for him. When Jesus said, "Follow me," to Peter for the last time, Peter knew he was pointing to a cross.

What kind of Calvary lies at the end of our journey is not ours to choose, and is rarely ours to know. It is enough for us to bear our own cross and come after him. To bear our cross means that whatever road we find ourselves on will be a Calvary Road of some kind, because our lives are being spent for the Master.

When we submitted to the waters of baptism, we were joining ourselves to Christ's death. Crucified with Christ, it is no longer we who live, but Christ who lives in us. And the Christ who lives in us teaches us how to carry a cross, how to lay down our lives.

People who observed Jesus dining with Simon the Pharisee or walking through the grain fields with his disciples on the Sabbath could have no idea that inwardly he was already carrying his cross. From the day Jesus emerged from his wilderness encounter with Satan the cross was there, planted in the depths of his soul. This cross released the power of the Spirit into the bodies of the sick and the eyes of the blind. Every day Jesus joyfully laid down his life for the sheep, pouring himself out in love, as he moved ever closer to his goal, where he would carry his cross no farther. It would carry him.

To follow Jesus is to follow him to a cross of our own. People who observe us driving down the road or feasting with our friends could have no idea that we carry a cross, that we are committed to laying down our lives in the service of our Master. But we are allowing the power of Christ's death to work in us, setting us free from ourselves, so that the life of Christ can flow out of us to others (see 2 Cor 4:10-12).

If you were looking at our friend Janice in the officers' mess, you would never have guessed that she was carrying a cross. Her husband was a high-ranking naval officer. She had a great sense of humor and appeared to be the life of the party. Yet, when someone's heart was breaking, Janice seemed to know what to do. When someone needed a place to stay, Janice's home was open. A financial crisis? Janice would be there with money. Few people even noticed that she was pouring herself out for people. She made it seem like nothing at all.

Janice's love for Jesus seemed almost matter-of-fact. But

beneath the surface, she carried a cross. She knew that her life was not her own; it belonged to the Master. It was to be spent, offered up. Janice willingly allowed the death of Jesus to work in her, so that the life of Jesus could flow from her. Only the angels know the power that flowed through this woman's life. A trail of miracles followed her, and she never looked back.

The day Jesus gave Peter the power of the keys was the day Jesus began laying on Peter the news that a cross lay ahead—not only for Jesus, but for Peter too. This was the day Jesus started teaching the disciples to take up a cross.

The keys of the kingdom and the cross that we carry are identical. When you see men or women who possess the power of the keys, you are looking at disciples possessed by an inward cross. They may look like beggars or kings, but they have been crucified with Christ. It is no longer they who live, but Christ who lives in them. And the life they now live in the flesh, they live by faith in the Son of God. By faith they follow in his steps. By faith they deny themselves, take up their cross daily, and bear it joyfully toward their appointed Calvaries. They may die peacefully in their own beds, but the lives they lived will have been poured out for others in praise to God. They were faithful unto death, whatever death God chose for them.

The Power of the Keys and the Mind of Christ

I caught myself thinking, Elsie will never change, and was convicted. How could I bring Christ's redemption to Elsie, when my mind had already tossed her in the recycling bin?

When Jesus looks into Elsie's soul, he sees her sins more

clearly than I do. But he also sees wounds and fears and despair that I cannot see. He loves this woman. He will not say of her in this age of grace, "Elsie will never change." He looks upon her with hope. He knows how close she has come, during those lonely nights, to saying, "I give up. Here I am, Lord. I'm yours."

Who is shaping my thinking about Elsie, when I say to myself, Elsie will never change? Certainly not the mind of Christ. When a spirit of cynicism shapes my thoughts about this woman, my mind is "conformed to this world," and the keys of the kingdom would be unsafe in my hands.

"Do not be conformed to this world but be transformed by the renewal of your mind, that you may prove what is the will of God, what is good and acceptable and perfect" (Rom 12:2). But I can choose to allow the Spirit of God to transform my thinking about this woman, so that I begin to regard her from Jesus' point of view. Instead of saying, "Elsie will never change," I see her against the background of the cross. What Jesus did for me, he also did for her. I repent of my judgment of this woman and discipline myself to pray God's richest blessings upon her.

The keys of the kingdom are only given to those who allow their thinking to be shaped by the mind of Christ. "To set the mind on the flesh [resentment, suspicion, lust, greed] is death, but to set the mind on the Spirit [Jesus] is life and peace" (Rom 8:6). To live in the dimension of the kingdom where all things are possible is to choose to live with a *transformed mind*, with thinking that is renewed by the Spirit of Christ day by day.

Keeping the Mind Focused

I remember watching an evangelist demonstrate how to "name it and claim it." His eyes shut tightly as he pictured the Learjet in his mind. He claimed it in the name of Jesus and described how he already saw himself cruising at 39,000 feet. Hallelujah! It was *his*, by faith, Hallelujah! Doesn't God want his children to travel first class? All things are possible to those who believe! Delight thyself in the Lord, and he shall give thee the desires of thine heart.

If the Lord is our supreme delight and the Learjet is some-how essential to our service to him—well, maybe. But we're on shaky ground when, as adult servants of God, our prayers are consumed with naming and claiming toys, or when money becomes the focus of our "vision."

Jesus' teachings about faith are given to disciples, committed followers. All things are possible for those who put the king-dom first. But to take Jesus' "faith principles" and turn them into a highway to prosperity and success, on this world's terms, is to imply that Jesus was wrong: that you can serve God *and* mammon at the same time. Every man or woman who takes that road will sooner or later end up a slave to mammon. Because the mind has lost its focus. It has become conformed to this world.

Jesus' Name, Jesus' Mind

"Hitherto you have asked nothing in my name; ask, and you will receive, that your joy may be full" (Jn 16:24).

"In the name of Jesus Christ of Nazareth, walk!" said Peter, as he grasped the man by the right hand and raised him up. How could this man, who had been lame from birth, suddenly begin to walk? Peter explained to the crowd that it was the name of Jesus, whom they had crucified, which had healed this man. "His name ... has made this man strong whom you see and know" (Acts 3:16).

To be able to use the name of Jesus with such power, to pray in Jesus' name and receive answers, presupposes that Peter and John had come into Jesus' mind. Their minds were at one with their Master's.

When the ambassador speaks in the name of the king, he speaks for the king. He expresses the king's mind. When the believer speaks (or prays) in the name of the Lord Jesus, he speaks for Jesus. He expresses the mind of Christ.

Merely tacking "in Jesus' name" to the end of our prayers does not, by itself, clothe them with the authority of Jesus. But when we have Jesus' mind, then we can speak in his name, pray in his name, for our words are in harmony with the mind of the Master. If Jesus' mind is set on a Learjet, then we should be able to pray with ease for a Learjet and a hangar to house it. But if Jesus' mind is elsewhere, our prayers and desires will follow his lead. If I pray in Jesus' name or even cast out demons in Jesus' name, without having Jesus' heart, Jesus' mind, I may one day have to hear him say, "I never knew you."

If You Abide in Me

Don't worry about producing miracles. Miracles will come by themselves. Signs of the kingdom will flow from your life as naturally as grapes form on the branch. The branch doesn't strive to produce grapes. The branch simply maintains a living connection with the vine. From the vine the branch receives power to breathe and drink in sunlight. Nourished by the life of the vine, grapes begin to form.

Our job is to stay focused on Jesus, to make sure that we are abiding in him and his words are being lived out by us. That's all we have to worry about. If we abide in Christ and he in us, we will bear fruit. We receive life from him as we keep our minds stayed on him. It's his program, not ours. All we do is fit into the program, as he makes it clear. He tells us that Elsie can change, and we believe him. He begins to put his finger on attitudes and murky regions of our own hearts, and calls us to repentance. And we obey him. He teaches us from within that the Father desires mercy and not sacrifice. He commands us to take the love which he pours into us, and start pouring it out toward each other, and toward all people.

As we keep bringing our hearts out of darkness into the light and yielding to his will, our fellowship with Jesus deepens. We are abiding in him, and he in us. We are exchanging our hearts of stone for his heart. His mind is being formed in us.

Ask Whatever You Will

You want the revival to spread? Ask for it, and it will be done for you. Don't be timid. Ask! Of course, there is the eternal condition: "if you abide in me and my words abide in you" (Jn 15:7). To abide is to dwell. To stay. To live in Christ—to eat, sleep and drink Jesus. To wake up in the night and bend our thoughts toward him. To rise in the morning and place our lives at his disposal. And to have his words abiding in us is to allow his words to reach our hearts before they fall out of our mouths. To trust his words to the point of obedience, even when it costs us.

"Forgive."

"Give to him who needs."

"Go, make disciples."

"Seek the kingdom first."

"Take up your cross daily."

"If I then, your Lord and teacher, have washed your feet, you also ought to wash one another's feet."

Jesus' words abide in us only by becoming incarnate in our flesh.

Who of us can presume to claim that Jesus' words are abiding in us without interference from our egos and our fleshly fears? Yet as we pursue the vision of what our Master expects us to be, help comes from above. The fire of heaven begins to burn out the dross and warm the fear-chilled corners of our hearts with hope. We pray, and the Lord himself prays within us. We ask what we will, and what we will begins to approach what he wills. Doors open. All things become possible.

Free the Captives

When a strong man, fully armed, guards his own palace, his goods are in peace; but when one stronger than he assails him and overcomes him, he takes away his armor in which he trusted, and divides his spoil. He who is not with me is against me, and he who does not gather with me scatters.

LUKE 11:21-23

Jesus entered Satan's "palace" when he came to this earth. He overcame Satan and removed his armor through his death on the cross. But millions are still prisoners of Satan's lies. They have yet to experience the redeeming power of the cross of Christ. "Are you with me?" says the Master. "He who is not with me is against me, and he who does not gather with me scatters" (Lk 11:23). Cleansed by Jesus' blood and revived by his Spirit, we are sent to free the captives: men and women who live near us, work next to us. Friends from school. Relatives. "As the Father has sent me, even so I send you" (Jn 20:21).

THIRTEEN

Hello, Lazarus!

Sooner or later, every revival is tested. If it survives the test, the revival is strengthened. If it fails, it begins to weaken and drift. One of the most difficult tests comes in the form of a human visitor, who hardly looks like a messenger of God. In fact, the man is a disruption. How can we concentrate on the glories of heaven-sent revival, when this repulsive beggar parks his infectious body right outside our door?

"We'd like to help you, friend, but you've come at a bad time. Our prayer service is about to begin."

"All I'm asking for is a little food. Or maybe money for a cup of coffee."

"Here's five dollars. Wish it could be more. See you later."

We breathe a sigh of relief as he walks away, but somehow we know that our prayer meeting is already off to a bad start. Could it be that there is a connection between revival and this needy man?

We first meet Lazarus in a parable of Jesus, lying at the rich man's gate, covered with sores and yearning for a few scraps from the rich man's table. Only the dogs seem to care about this man, as they come and lick his sores. But heaven is watching over Lazarus. Lazarus dies, and a band of angels carries him to Abraham's bosom.

The rich man also dies and finds himself in a place of anguish. Looking up toward heaven, the rich man sees Lazarus from afar, resting in the bosom of Abraham. Strange, during his earthly life, when Lazarus lay at his gate, the rich man never noticed him. But now he even remembers the beggar's name. "Father Abraham, have mercy upon me, and send Lazarus to dip the end of his finger in water and cool my tongue; for I am in anguish in this flame" (Lk 16:24).

There was a time when Lazarus could have done much more than ease the rich man's pain. Lazarus could have been the doorway to the rich man's spiritual awakening. It was no accident that he lay begging at this particular gate. In the mysterious workings of God's mercy, Lazarus lay there as the rich man's hope.

Through Lazarus, God was offering the rich man a way to redeem his covetous soul. Show Lazarus a little kindness, offer him a little relief from his suffering, and you are learning mercy, opening the door of your heart to receive the gift of grace.

How can a heart of stone receive grace? Talk to Lazarus. Put some salve on those wounds, bring him some bread and wine to give him strength. Fill his empty pocket with a bit of money out of your abundance. The encouragement you give to Lazarus will multiply a thousand times over in your own heart, and you will begin to hear the voice of God once more.

The rich man was no heathen. He kept the Sabbath. He faithfully attended the synagogue and always journeyed to Jerusalem for the high holy days. But he saw no connection between his faith and this miserable beggar at his gate. The rich man was blind. He could not see that Lazarus was his link with the living God.

Welcome Lazarus, and you welcome the Messiah. Reject Lazarus, and you have rejected the Messiah, no matter how fervent your prayers or eloquent your witness.

What's the Connection?

If there is a connection between revival and the appearance of Lazarus in our lives, it is one that is often hard to fathom. Lazarus neither looks nor acts like a gift from God. He is repulsive, disruptive, demanding, ungrateful, and he seems to have an intuitive sense of the most inopportune time to appear.

Sometimes Lazarus is bold enough to come in and worship with us. Before long we can see that we have a problem on our hands. This person sets everybody on edge. You never know what he or she is going to come out with. He can throw a meeting off balance in thirty seconds. And even when she sits and stares at the ceiling, she seems to drain the life out of us. What can such a person possibly contribute to the revival among us?

Our encounter with Lazarus begins with the best of intentions. After all, revival has inspired us to "rejoice in the Lord always"—in all circumstances. We find ourselves praising God for the blue sky and the green grass, for the snow, and the wind and the rain beating against the window.

Rejoice in the Lord always; again I will say, Rejoice. Let all men know your forbearance. The Lord is at hand. Have no anxiety about anything, but in everything by prayer and supplication with thanksgiving let your requests be made known to God.

PHILIPPIANS 4:4-6

Our hearts open wide to people we formerly held at a distance. Welcome, Lazarus! The Lord is so good! Come in and enjoy his goodness with us!

But soon our generosity is challenged. Lazarus begins to manifest his true nature. Instead of showing grateful appreciation for our kindness, he starts biting the hand that feeds him. He complains. He insults half the people at the potluck. And the Spirit reminds us that this is our opportunity to "let all men know your forbearance [the generous overlooking of insult or injury]." We are being shown by the Lord that revival is not just ecstasy and joy, it is also forgiveness, forbearance, patience, faithfulness toward "difficult" people, as God has been faithful to us.

But where will it all lead? We seem to have a bull in our china shop that needs a tranquilizing bullet.

No, says the Spirit, you have a living soul in your midst for whom the Lamb's blood was shed as truly as it was shed for you. How you treat this person has more to do than you may imagine with how the revival among you will progress. "Have no anxiety about anything, but in everything by prayer and supplication with thanksgiving let your requests be made known to God."

Throughout our Lord's ministry there was always a Lazarus near him. By example, Jesus taught his disciples the importance of treating Lazarus with honor and love. Each Lazarus was sent by God. And each Lazarus who drew near to Jesus was a type, a foreshadowing, of a person whom we can expect to meet, as revival spreads among us. We need to look very carefully at these "Lazaruses" who came to Jesus, and observe how Jesus treated each one. For if Lazarus is not already among us, he soon will be. He comes to us as a gift from God and is to be treated as such.

Meet the Woman at the Well

> There came a woman of Samaria to draw water. Jesus said to her, "Give me a drink." For his disciples had gone away into the city to buy food. The Samaritan woman said to him, "How is it that you, a Jew, ask a drink of me, a woman of Samaria?"
>
> JOHN 4:7-9

Don't expect this woman to come knocking at the door of your church, looking for salvation. She is very conscious of being a "Samaritan," an outsider, and she has no interest in finding acceptance in your church. Yet she carries a water jar that needs to be filled. She's thirsty. And she brings with her a history of many disappointments. Now she approaches the well, a public place, where everybody in the village comes for water. She chooses to come at high noon, an hour when the well is normally deserted.

The important thing for us to remember is that this woman has been sent across our path by the living God. Our love for God is confirmed or invalidated by the way we regard her, the way we relate to her.

Jesus knows that he is on her turf. This is her well, not his. He is her guest. "Give me a drink."

"How is it that you, a Jew, ask a drink of me, a woman of Samaria?" (You're a Jew; I'm a Samaritan. You're a man, I'm a woman. You shouldn't be talking to me. And I shouldn't be talking to you.)

"If you knew what God has in store for you, and who it is that's asking you for a drink, you would have asked him and he would have given you living water."

"Living water? Where are you going to get that? Are you greater than our father Jacob, who gave us this well?"

"Whoever drinks of this water will thirst again, but whoever drinks of the water that I give him will never thirst. The water that I give will become a spring within him, welling up to eternal life."

"Okay, give me this water."

"Go call your husband and come here."

"I have no husband."

"You've had five husbands, and the one you have now is not your husband."

"I can see you're a prophet. So where's the right place to worship? You say Jerusalem. We say this mountain."

"Believe me, woman, neither this mountain nor Jerusalem is the place. The hour is coming—has come—when true worshipers will worship the Father in spirit and in truth."

"Well, I know that when Messiah comes, he'll show us."

"You're looking at him."

The woman leaves her water jar at the well and returns to the village with a gospel. "Come, see a man who told me all I ever did. Is not this the Messiah?" Her words ignite the village and they follow her to the Master.

This woman can be found in every city on earth and in every country village. Not only is she thirsty for living water, she is a window through which the encouragement of heaven visits every disciple who asks her for a drink. This woman may be living next door to us. She may work where we work.

The woman at the well cannot be reached with a canned gospel. She's real. She's down-to-earth. She knows more about life than we do and can smell a patronizing attitude ten miles away. But she is open to the truth, when she hears it spoken and sees it lived. Sooner or later, because she is thirsty, God will guide her to the living water. But if we walk past her in our blindness or drive her away with our arrogance, we quench the flame God has ignited within us.

Look for Levi the Tax Collector

As he passed on, he saw Levi the son of Alphaeus sitting at the tax office, and he said to him, "Follow me." And he rose and followed him. And as he sat at table in his house, many tax collectors and sinners were sitting with Jesus and his disciples.

MARK 2:14-15

Levi too is an outsider. He tries not to let it bother him. He keeps himself busy doing what he does best: making money. Respectable people shun Levi. It irks them that Levi has a bigger house than they do. That Levi sends his children to better schools, eats better, dresses better. Levi is a man of the world. What do we have in common with Levi? Let him do his thing, and we'll get on with the business of the kingdom of God.

But Jesus doesn't see it that way. Jesus looks at Levi and sees a rich man who isn't nearly as attached to things as many respectable believers are. Levi may know the value of money, but he also knows its limits. This man is closer to the kingdom than his critics would ever dream, because he at least regards himself as a sinner in need of redemption. He's poor in spirit.

Levi hasn't been spending all his time in the tax office. More than once Jesus has noticed him standing on the edge of the crowd, listening, watching the healings with tears running down his face. This man is ready to be a disciple.

Jesus never singles him out of the crowd. He waits until he finds Levi on his own turf, his tax office. "Follow me." Jesus only has to say it once.

Levi knows what this means. He's been hoping for this moment. He gets up and follows. Levi's first response is to invite all his friends to celebrate with him, as he begins his new life with the Master.

My friend Ray was born knowing how to survive and how to "make a buck." In the days when he owned a bar near Tiger Stadium, few people would have dreamed that this man, who always carried a handgun in his belt and knew how to use it, was on a quest for the kingdom of God.

When Ray saw some of his friends committing their lives to Jesus, he envied them. Part of him wanted to join them. But *what about all the changes I'll have to make, if I turn my life over to Jesus?* The inner wrestling match went on for several years.

Then one hot July evening a soft-spoken Jewish woman who

loves Jesus came for a chat. Soon the word was out that Ray had done it. He was following Jesus.

There were people who came to our church just to see if it was true that Ray was "going to church." But he did more than go to church. He began making changes in the way he lived. He sold the bar. He began giving instead of taking. And to the amazement of most of his friends, Ray unashamedly announced to all who would listen that Jesus was the one who was changing his life.

Don't be misled by Levi's worldly appearance. Something holy is at work within him. He is a window through which the encouragement of heaven descends upon those who reach out to welcome him. Find him. Get to know him. Meet him on his own turf. Watch the Spirit of God move on him ... and on you, as you serve him in Jesus' name.

Welcome Mary Magdalene

And the twelve were with him, and also some women who had been healed of evil spirits and infirmities: Mary, called Magdalene, from whom seven devils had gone out, and Joanna, the wife of Chuza, Herod's steward, and Susanna, and many others, who provided for them out of their means.

LUKE 8:1-3

When the disciples first saw Mary Magdalene, she was a basket case. "Send her away, Master, she disrupts our meetings with her crying and carrying on. If she keeps coming, everybody else will leave."

But Jesus saw Mary Magdalene with different eyes. He saw a

tender spirit, crushed beneath the weight of demonic chains. Seven devils had found their way into this suffering soul. The last thing this woman needed was another rejection.

"Mary," he said to her. She ceased her sobbing and gazed at him through veiled eyes. She could not speak. Her face turned toward the door. Should she make a run for it?

"Mary," he said a second time. Her seven captors were still holding her hostage. Then came the word of command from the Master. Ordered to depart, these spirits of despair slid from her soul like seven serpents alarmed by a sudden light.

A few years later she would hear her name spoken from his lips, when everyone thought he was dead. "Mary," he would say. She would be the first to see him and talk with him.

Meanwhile, Mary Magdalene, who seemed so unpromising when they first met her, became a major force in that band of followers. She poured out her life in gratitude for her deliverance. She served. She provided for them out of her means. She is remembered to this day as a daughter of encouragement in the ministry of our Lord.

And God will use Mary Magdalene to teach us vital lessons, if we will allow our eyes to see beyond her misery. We're looking at a person who has a troubled mind. She walks into the room and people become uncomfortable. Was it just in apostolic times that a person like Mary Magdalene could be delivered from her demons? Is it absurd to expect the Lord in our midst to set this woman free? Surely someone among us has eyes to see the tender spirit crushed under those chains.

But what's the procedure? How do we deal with this

woman? Do we place her on a chair in the middle of the room and start rebuking her demons?

Don't worry about the procedure. Jesus never offered a seminar on how to cast out demons. He just gave his followers authority over the dark spirits, trusting that when the need arose, they would know what to do. "Heal the sick, cast out demons," Jesus said, as he sent them out in his name. But Jesus had a lot to say about the kind of love that welcomes people and heals their souls. Love that forgives, forbears, takes time with people, treats them with honor, washes their feet.

If we welcome Mary Magdalene who comes to us with a troubled spirit, if we accept her, treat her with respect, love her, God will show us what she needs. And as we welcome her, the revival will gain strength.

Appreciate Zacchaeus

And there was a man named Zacchaeus; he was a chief tax collector, and rich. And he sought to see who Jesus was, but could not, on account of the crowd, because he was small of stature. So he ran on ahead and climbed up into a sycamore tree to see him, for he was to pass that way. And when Jesus came to the place, he looked up and said to him, "Zacchaeus, make haste and come down; for I must stay at your house today."

LUKE 19:2-5

God sends Zacchaeus into our lives to teach us humility. "Whoever exalts himself will be humbled, and whoever humbles himself will be exalted" (Mt 23:12). Zacchaeus finds it easy to respond to Jesus because he knows how to humble himself.

People murmured when Jesus went to have dinner with Zacchaeus. "He has gone to be the guest of a man who is a sinner." True, Zacchaeus knew how to clip off a healthy share for himself when he collected taxes for his Roman masters. But he also knew that his soul was empty. When Zacchaeus spotted the crowd coming down the road, pressing around the Galilean prophet, it brought a flash of hope. This rich little tax collector threw his pride out the window, ran ahead and climbed a tree.

"Look at Zacchaeus, up in that sycamore tree!" people snickered.

He didn't care. He wanted to see Jesus.

"Zacchaeus, hurry up and come down; for I must stay at your house today," said Jesus.

Pride would have run away, covered with embarrassment. Zacchaeus scrambled down and received Jesus joyfully.

In the middle of dinner, Zacchaeus stood up and took a step of repentance and faith, in the one way that made sense to him. "Behold, Lord, the half of my goods I will now give to the poor. And if I have defrauded any one of anything, I restore it fourfold."

Jesus asked nothing more and said, "Today, salvation has come to this house" (Lk 19:8-9).

Was Zacchaeus buying salvation by giving half his goods to the poor? No, this was Zacchaeus' response to the salvation that came to him when Jesus entered his house. Zacchaeus was grateful to the point where he opened his heart and offered up to God the wealth that had always meant so much to him.

When Zacchaeus finds his way into our church, we become uncomfortable with the way he casts aside his pride and throws away his money. We're convicted. Because we know that the revival which has ignited us is calling us to follow his example.

Lord, help us to lay aside our pride as easily as this man does; and enable us, like Zacchaeus, to loose our grip on mammon!

Don't Send Her Away!

And behold a Canaanite woman from that region came out and cried, "Have mercy on me, O Lord, Son of David; my daughter is severely possessed by a demon." But he did not answer her a word. And his disciples came and begged him, saying, "Send her away, for she is crying after us."

MATTHEW 15:22-23

She's a Canaanite. The faithful regard her as a Gentile dog. You don't take the children's bread and throw it to dogs. She's aggressive. She's loud. She has a one-track mind. Send her away. Please, Master, get rid of her!

Sometimes this Canaanite woman worms her way into our churches and causes havoc. She mars our Bible studies, she throws a wrench into our planning meetings with her one-track mind. If she's spotted before she reaches the front door, three ushers are there to meet her and turn her away, before she disrupts the service.

What does she want? Why is she making such a fuss?

Jesus acts as if he couldn't care less about the woman's need. "I was sent only to the lost sheep of the house of Israel."

But she comes and kneels before him, "Lord, help me."

"It's not fair to take the children's bread and throw it to dogs," says the Master.

"Yes, Lord, yet even the dogs eat the crumbs that fall from their master's table."

At last Jesus reveals his heart. "O woman, great is your faith! Be it done for you as you desire." And her daughter is healed instantly.

Don't send her away. Listen to her. Give her a chance to express the cry of her soul. If she wants to talk during the service, bring her into another room and talk with her. She was sent to us by God. Meet her in his name. Respond to her with his love, and the fire of heaven will begin to answer her cry and overflow from her grateful heart.

One day I saw a middle-aged woman sitting on the church steps, drinking from a two-liter bottle of Pepsi. "Caught me drinking on the church steps." She chuckled.

I invited her to come in, but she wasn't comfortable with the idea. The invitation must have haunted her, because a few months later, there she was, sitting in the back of the church, jotting down on paper her critique of everything she observed.

Joan had an active (some would say overactive) mind. And her mouth never lagged far behind. At Bible studies she delighted in "stealing the show" with a barrage of questions and comments that blasted away all tranquillity. "Why does God let babies suffer? Why don't churches practice what they preach? What makes you people think you have all the answers?" Twice I felt that Joan was going too far on her "campaign of disruption" and sent her away as if she were a naughty child. Both times Joan was deeply hurt, and I was far from comfortable with myself or with the Lord. It seemed that when Joan left, things became too quiet. It was an empty quiet, a disturbing quiet. Did something of the Spirit of God leave with her?

Well, what else could I do? I asked myself. What else, indeed.

I would visit Joan, and we would agree on some ground rules. On her return, Joan would push the rules to the limit. But we knew that we were stuck with each other. Joan belonged to us, and we belonged to her. The Lord had brought us together for some refining. She too is part of the revival.

What's This Samaritan Doing Here?

And as he entered a village, he was met by ten lepers, who stood at a distance and lifted up their voices and said, "Jesus, Master, have mercy on us." When he saw them he said to them, "Go and show yourselves to the priests." And as they went they were cleansed. Then one of them, when he saw that he was healed, turned back, praising God with a loud voice; and he fell on his face at Jesus' feet, giving him thanks. Now he was a Samaritan.

LUKE 17:12-16

The Samaritan is the supreme outsider. He belongs to a nation in our midst that frightens us. Samaritans are sullen and angry. You never know what's going on in their heads. Yet, most of us have received more kindness from Samaritans than we like to admit. When you couldn't figure out which subway would get you to the Bronx, a Samaritan went out of his way to put you on the right train. When your car broke down outside Philadelphia, a Samaritan came to your rescue. Was there anyone at the time of your bereavement who brought more warmth and comfort than a Samaritan mother who fed you in her kitchen and called you often to see how you were doing?

But why is this Samaritan coming to our church? Doesn't he have a church of his own? What's he up to?

He probably couldn't explain it himself. All he knows is that he has come here with a full heart, a grateful heart. He wants to fall on his face at Jesus' feet and give thanks. Can't we see that this Samaritan brings with him a spirit of gratefulness that we badly need? As he lifts his heart in thanksgiving, we are lifted with him. And the Spirit within us says, "Learn from this man. He knows how to appreciate what God has done for him. And he's not afraid to express it."

One Sunday Billie and her mother, Alice, were driving past our church and noticed some black people coming out, along with the white folks.

"I guess we'd be welcomed there," said Billie. "It's only half as far as we're driving now. Let's try it next Sunday."

Billie and Alice came, felt comfortable and were soon part of the congregation.

Alice liked to praise God. She liked to say, "Hallelujah! Thank you, Jesus!" when her heart overflowed. But Messiah Church, in those days, was rather subdued. Nobody said "Hallelujah! Thank you, Jesus!" unless the words were properly expressed as part of the liturgy. The first time it happened, Billie could tell that some of the worshipers were disturbed.

"Better cool it, Mama," said Billie, "We're new here."

I can still remember Alice's smile, as she said to her daughter, "If I want to praise my God, I'm going to praise my God!" In a few years the congregation began to catch up with Alice's spirit of praise and thanksgiving.

Nicodemus

He doesn't look like a Lazarus. He seems to have it together. Well educated, financially secure, highly respected in the community. He's the kind of man any church is proud to have as a member. If we play it right, Nicodemus will bring a flood of followers with him. "Nicodemus joined that church? Wow! Maybe we should check it out." Get Nicodemus, and you'll get his constituents.

Our temptation is to roll out the red carpet for Nicodemus, to exploit his high standing in the community in the service of the revival. If we succumb to this temptation, Nicodemus will suffer, and so will the revival.

Now there was a man of the Pharisees, named Nicodemus, a ruler of the Jews. This man came to Jesus by night and said to him, "Rabbi, we know that you are a teacher come from God; for no one can do these signs that you do, unless God is with him." Jesus answered him, "Truly, truly, I say to you, unless one is born anew, he cannot see the kingdom of God."

JOHN 3:1-3

"Unless one is born anew, he cannot see the kingdom of God." What a strange welcome for this high-profile visitor!

People have always treated Nicodemus as one of Israel's best. Why does Jesus tell this fine man that he needs to be born anew?

Nicodemus knows that something is missing in his soul. But surely it's only a matter of upgrading. He has come to Jesus looking for the missing piece that will complete him.

But even if you're a respected Nicodemus, you don't need an upgrade, you need a rebirth. You need to discover that the nature you were born with, even at its very best, is twisted in upon itself. It watches itself performing those acts of piety with satisfaction. It stands outside itself and admires its charity and good sense. People come for advice and go away singing your praises. And these very praises cling to the walls of your soul like trophies won in a tournament, and blind you to the truth about yourself, until the Master explains to you that that which is born of the flesh is flesh. You need to be born of the Spirit.

This is why Jesus received Nicodemus, not as a celebrity, but as a Lazarus. Jesus saw the need of his soul and put it under the light of heaven, so that Nicodemus could see it too. This frustrating interview was the turning point in the man's life.

When the local magistrate began attending our church in Nova Scotia, it was soon the talk of the town. The magistrate had not been inside a church for many a year, and he was hardly thought of as a religious man. But he had power, and that power was respected. Shortly after he had donated a stove for our kitchen, the magistrate joined the men of the church for a supper of fish chowder. Perhaps he was disappointed that these younger, less educated men treated him as a peer. After all, he was the magistrate. And some of these very men had appeared as defendants in his court. To add to his discomfort, the speaker delivered a strong, pointed message. The magistrate was offended. He noisily pushed back his chair and made for the door.

Two men followed the magistrate to the narthex and challenged him, in the name of the Lord, to "stick around, and be a brother." He hesitated, sighed and returned to his seat. For his own good, this man was to be loved, but not coddled.

Nicodemus reappears twice more on the pages of the Gospel of John. Each time his faith appears to be stronger. After the crucifixion we see Nicodemus lugging a chest of costly spices for Jesus' burial, risking his reputation as a teacher in Israel, clear evidence that he has now become a disciple.

When Nicodemus comes to our church, he needs to be loved, but not catered to. After he receives his rebirth, give him a chance to walk humbly with his Lord. Don't turn the spotlight on him for the world to see and call it his "testimony." That's exploitation and may very well endanger the new life which has begun in him. If we welcome Nicodemus the way Jesus welcomed him, keeping it low-key and concentrating on the one need of his soul—rebirth—then the cry of his heart will find a genuine answer.

Passing the Test

Lazarus is not a distraction. He is an essential part of every revival. Through this needy person, Jesus is saying to the potential Pharisee within each of us, "Go and learn what this means, 'I desire mercy, and not sacrifice'" (Mt 9:13). Mercy is learned, not through contemplation, but through practice—in dealing with real people with real needs, who try our patience in unexpected ways.

As our revival passes the "Lazarus test," it acquires flesh-and-blood hands and feet and begins to travel beyond the walls of our homes and churches into places that were heretofore untouched by it. We will watch in amazement, as the Lord adds to our number day by day those who are being saved (see Acts 2:47).

FOURTEEN

Fresh Wineskins

Who ever heard of a stale revival? One of the primary marks of a revival is its life, its immediacy. Suddenly everybody is conscious that God is among us. Jesus, the Crucified, is risen and alive in our midst! His word is convicting our hearts, bringing us to repentance and breaking chains that have held us captive for years. But will this freshness last? After all, everything in our world seems to harden and crumble with the passing of time. Our bodies age. Our bones become brittle.

When Jesus pours new wine into fresh wineskins, as he does in every revival, he expects the wineskins to remain fresh. The new wine of his word never ages. And that word has the power to keep us fresh: "So we do not lose heart. Though our outer nature is wasting away, our inner nature is being renewed every day" (2 Cor 4:16).

Paul's wineskin remained fresh because he knew how to participate in a daily revival. He allowed the word of his Master to renew him day by day. And our wineskins will do the same as long as we make sure they are filled only with new wine—Jesus' word.

But what happens to many believers is that after a while they begin mixing a bit of old wine with the new. Old wine is any religious idea or practice that we substitute for a personal, obedient relationship with Jesus. For instance, if you find yourself evaluating believers on the basis of their view of the rapture, the formula they use to baptize people or whether their approach to prayer is the same as yours, you have begun mixing old wine with the new. And that old wine (of fleshly religion) will cause your wineskin to harden. If you can look at a woman and identify the depth of her commitment to Jesus by her jewelry, you have begun mixing old wine with the new. Your wineskin is becoming brittle.

Caiaphas, the high priest, was looking for the Messiah. Since his childhood Caiaphas had prayed that the Messiah would come in his lifetime. He was expectant.

When John the Baptist burst on the scene, Caiaphas was curious. Scouts were sent to question him.

"Are you the Messiah?"

"No."

"Are you Elijah?"

"No."

"Are you the prophet Moses foretold?"

"No."

"Well then, who are you? Give us an answer for those who sent us."

"I am the voice of one crying in the wilderness, 'Make straight the way of the Lord'" (Jn 1:23).

Caiaphas heard about Jesus, the Nazarene, how he healed the sick and cast out demons. But how could he be the Messiah? He healed people on the Sabbath. He ate with tax collectors and sinners. He didn't purify his hands before the meal.

The scouts came in for a closer look, just as Jesus was having dinner with Levi the tax collector. "Why do you eat with tax collectors and sinners? And how come the disciples of John fast and offer prayers, and so do the disciples of the Pharisees, but your disciples eat and drink?"

"And Jesus said to them, 'Can you make the wedding guests fast while the bridegroom is with them? The days will come, when the bridegroom is taken away from them, and then they will fast in those days.... No one puts new wine into old wineskins; if he does, the new wine will burst the skins and it will be spilled, and the skins will be destroyed. But new wine must be put into fresh wineskins'" (Lk 5:34-35, 37-38).

Caiaphas, the high priest, prayed for the Messiah to come. When at last the Messiah stood before him, Caiaphas sent him to his death. Caiaphas was an old wineskin. He could not handle the new wine.

There was a man named Cleopas. He too was looking for the Messiah. When Cleopas met Jesus, he saw what Caiaphas could not see. He saw light as he watched Jesus heal the sick, bring good news to the poor and call sinners to repentance. Convinced that this was the Messiah, he threw in his lot with Jesus and followed him.

Then it all fell apart. Thursday night Jesus was arrested by the temple police. Friday morning Caiaphas turned him over to Pilate to be killed. Now it's Sunday evening, and Cleopas and a friend are on their way to Emmaus to get away for a while. A stranger joins them on the road, listens to their conversation.

"Why are you so upset?" he asks.

"Haven't you heard the things that went on in Jerusalem this Passover?"

"What things?"

"Concerning Jesus of Nazareth, how our priests and rulers had him condemned to death and crucified. But we had hoped that he was the one to redeem Israel."

"O foolish men, and slow of heart to believe all that the prophets have spoken! Was it not necessary that the Messiah should suffer these things and enter into his glory?"

Now they draw near the village. The stranger appears to be going further. "Stay with us, for it is toward evening and the day is now far spent." They sit down to eat. The stranger takes the bread, blesses it, breaks it and gives it to them. And their eyes are opened, and they recognize him (see Lk 24:13-31).

Caiaphas met the Messiah and sent him to his death. Cleopas met a stranger on the road, who spoke the living word to him. Cleopas welcomed that word into his heart and met the risen Lord. Caiaphas was an old wineskin. Cleopas was a fresh wineskin.

An old wineskin is religious. It may fast and pray and adhere to all the rules that old wineskins love. But it will not listen to the Messiah's call for repentance. It hardens its religious heart against the living Word. To the old wineskin all Jesus can say is, "Go and learn what this means, 'I desire mercy, and not sacrifice'" (Mt 9:13).

A fresh wineskin is tender toward the Word. It humbles itself and becomes like a child before the Master. It is quick to confess its sin and to repent. It obeys when the Master commands it to give and forgive and show mercy.

As the new wine of the kingdom begins to flow in our

revival, it searches for fresh wineskins. Old wineskins cannot contain it.

But surely God can see that we are fresh wineskins. Haven't we been praying for this revival for years? Haven't we committed ourselves to serving this revival in any way that God may choose to use us?

Yet, there lives in each of us a Caiaphas, as well as a Cleopas. The Caiaphas in us is looking for the Messiah to come as fire from heaven, but he has a fixed idea of how this is to happen. Our Caiaphas may be "Spirit filled" and acquainted with every move of God across the land. He knows for sure that the Spirit of God cannot possibly be alive in that primly dressed little man with every hair in place, adorned with a spotless clerical collar.

The little man in the clerical collar stands up to speak. His voice is thin. His hands are trembling. You mean we're going to have to sit through an hour of this? The Caiaphas in us is only half attentive, while the woman in front of us starts to sob. Come now, she must have a problem. Across the aisle old stone-face begins to rock like a pious Hasid.

The atmosphere around us is charged with the presence of God, as a living word pours from the mouth of the prim little man in the clerical collar. But we are deaf to it, because the Caiaphas within us has succeeded in hardening our hearts into brittle wineskins that measure people by standards which have nothing to do with the kingdom of God.

A wineskin remains fresh by constant vigilance. The Caiaphas in us must give place to Cleopas, as we repeatedly choose, with an act of the will, to repent and become children before the Master. We need to make sure that we put only new wine in our wineskins: his word. "If you continue in my word, you are truly my disciples, and you will know the truth, and the truth will make you free" (Jn 8:31-32).

Paul's letter to the Galatians was written to keep their wineskins fresh. Paul had given the Galatian believers the new wine of Jesus' gospel. But other teachers had come into those churches and were adding "works of the law" to the gospel of grace. Paul used extreme language to warn these men and women about what was happening to them. "O foolish Galatians! Who has bewitched you, before whose eyes Jesus Christ was publicly portrayed as crucified? Let me ask you only this: Did you receive the Spirit by the works of the law, or by hearing with faith? Are you so foolish? Having begun with the Spirit, are you now ending with the flesh?" (Gal 3:1-3).

The book of Galatians is a timeless word of warning to wineskins that have made the mistake of mixing some old wine with the new: don't add anything to the gospel of grace in Jesus Christ. Don't substitute tradition, church work, Christian activism or anything else for simple obedience to the commands of Jesus.

Every one then who hears these words of mine and *does* them will be like a wise man who built his house upon the rock.

MATTHEW 7:24, emphasis added

And he was told, "Your mother and your brothers are standing outside, desiring to see you." But he said to them, "My mother and my brothers are those who hear the word of God and *do* it."

LUKE 8:20-21, emphasis added

There is no reason why we should not remain fresh the rest of our days on earth. Jesus' words are Spirit and life. All we have to do is keep listening to them and walking in them day by day.

FIFTEEN

A Worldwide Wake-Up Call

We began this book by focusing on the most important revival of your life: yours. The opening chapters were devoted to encouraging you to prepare the way for the Spirit of God to give you a new heredity, so that, washed in the Lamb's blood, you are no longer limited by your past, by the constraints of human flesh or by sin. We noted how the fire of heaven, released upon this earth through the death and resurrection of Jesus, desires to ignite your heart with power to continue the ministry which Jesus began. As your heart catches fire, Jesus passes on his "mantle," the Holy Spirit, to you and anoints you to bring good news to the poor, deliverance to the captives, sight to the blind and freedom to the oppressed.

In the second part of this book we considered how every personal revival is destined to spread to others and become part of something larger than itself. The flame within you reaches out to the flame in others, and soon signs of revival break out in your church, your prayer group, your circle of friends. As the cloud of glory once filled the ancient tabernacle, the atmosphere of heaven enters the assembly, and people are renewed. Enemies are reconciled. Healings occur. Praise and thanksgiving rise up toward the throne, and a spirit of welcome flows out to the broken lives beyond the walls. Jesus is lifted up before their eyes as crucified, and people are drawn to him.

Now, as we bring this book to a close, it is time to look at the larger picture. To see where all these streams of revival, which are presently flowing on every continent, are leading. Every revival which has occurred during the last twenty centuries has been a foretaste of something still to come. In each revival the Spirit is saying, "I am giving you a taste of the spiritual awakening that will one day cover this earth."

During the rapid breakdown in world order which will precede the close of the age, there will be a spiritual awakening such as this earth has never seen. I'm not talking about "gospel satellites" or mass-media wizardry. I'm talking about a grassroots, street-level move of the Spirit involving vast numbers of ordinary people whose hearts have been ignited with the fire of God. Initiated, ruled and directed, not by human strategists, but by the Spirit of God, this final worldwide spiritual awakening will leave the human race without excuse.

As the citizens of Wales, in its historic revival of 1904, were briefly torn from their normal lives and forced to face the living God and the crucified and risen Messiah, so the nations of earth will have their moment of revelation. They will stand exposed to a light that has come, not to judge them, but to call them one last time to turn and receive mercy. "For the earth will be filled with the knowledge of the glory of the Lord, as the waters cover the sea" (Heb 2:14). "And this gospel of the kingdom will be preached throughout the whole world, as a testimony to all nations; and then the end will come" (Mt 24:14).

Only the Father knows how the present, slowly spreading revival fits into his plan of salvation history. But we can be sure that this revival is moving us closer to that final worldwide wake-up call.

Keep in mind that you are an integral part of God's redemptive purpose. Behind the revival which has visited your life is Jesus himself, seeking to draw you into the center of God's will and make you ever more effective. The Spirit of God will accomplish through you far more than you would dare to imagine, if you will remember to fit into the program—God's program. Here are some things to consider:

The revival we are concerned with is God's revival, not man's. Jesus' warnings about false prophets, wolves in sheep's clothing, apply with striking accuracy wherever the Spirit begins to renew the body of Christ.

We need to be aware that for every genuine, God-initiated revival, there will usually be one or two counterfeit revivals nearby. The nearer we come to the end of the age, the more we can expect Jesus' warnings about false prophets and false Christs to apply. "You will know them by their fruits," says the Master (Mt 7:16). We are responsible to distinguish the difference between life that flows from the cross of Jesus and produces the fruit of genuine love, integrity, humility—and the humanly generated (often demonically inspired) "spirituality" that produces only bad fruit when the hoopla ends.

Does this revival bear the marks of Jesus Christ? Is it going about things the way he went about things? Can you picture Jesus pitching for money? Throwing his influence behind a particular political candidate? Leading a demonstration in front of the capitol in support of either the political left or the political right? What kind of followers is this revival producing? Are they humble disciples of Jesus? Or are they groupies?

We need to take seriously Jesus' warnings: "Beware of false prophets, who come to you in sheep's clothing but inwardly are ravenous wolves" (Mt 7:15). "Take heed that no one leads you astray" (Mt 24:4). "Then if any one says to you, 'Lo, here is the Christ!' or 'There he is!' do not believe it" (Mt 24:23).

Not every "revival" is God-initiated. And not every revival that begins with Jesus remains faithful to him. It is up to us to stay true to God's program for revival and commit our lives to his program alone.

At the same time, while we give false prophets a wide berth, our hearts are open to sisters and brothers from other branches of God's revival that may be very different from ours. Their worship may seem strange to us. They may hold different views about last things or how baptism is to be performed or who is an apostle and who isn't. But their love for Jesus is so obvious, the fruit of their lives is so clearly flowing from the cross of Christ, that we welcome them as fellow heirs in the kingdom. We and they are ruled by the same Spirit, living under the shadow of the same cross.

John and some of the other disciples were disturbed to find a man whom they did not know casting out demons in Jesus' name. "What do you think you're doing? Who gave you the right to cast out demons in Jesus' name? You are not one of us!" But when John told Jesus what they did, he said, "'Do not forbid him; for no one who does a mighty work in my name will be able soon after to speak evil of me. For he that is not against us is for us" (Mk 9:39-40).

God's program for revival is revealed in Jesus and centered on his cross. We pointed out in the first chapter of this book that God's program for revival is revealed in the way Jesus went about doing things. The Son emptied himself of his glory, became one of us and laid down his life for our redemption. Rising from the dead as the firstborn of the new creation, Jesus poured out the life of the Holy Spirit upon his followers. He set their hearts on fire with the fire of the Spirit of God.

The revival Jesus brings to us is consistent with the pattern of his life among us. We too are called to empty ourselves of our pride and nail our lives to Jesus' cross. We too are raised into a resurrection life by the power of the Holy Spirit so that we can serve the Father in the same way our Lord Jesus did.

Jesus never promoted himself, so we never promote ourselves.

Jesus used no gimmicks. We use no gimmicks.

Jesus never wasted time "raising funds," so we follow his example, trusting the Father to provide for us as we seek to do his will.

Jesus looked only to the Father for every word he spoke, every deed he performed. We look only to him. Not Jesus plus Moses, or Elijah, or the rapture, or this or that spiritual manifestation. Not Jesus plus our insights into the New Testament Church. Just Jesus.

Jesus depended on the Spirit to reveal the Father's will hour by hour. We do the same.

Jesus denied himself, took up his cross daily and pressed on toward Calvary. He commands us to do the same.

Jesus concentrated on fulfilling Isaiah 61:1-2.

The Spirit of the Lord is upon me, because he has anointed me to preach good news to the poor. He has sent me to proclaim release to the captives and recovering of sight to the blind, to set at liberty those who are oppressed, to proclaim the acceptable year of the Lord.

LUKE 4:18-19

Revival has come to us to empower us to fulfill this prophecy in Jesus' name by the power of his Spirit. We have been revived to bring Jesus' life to others—many others.

The goal of God's revival is a worldwide wake-up call. The Welsh Revival, like other revivals before and since, was a brief, brilliant flash of glory. For a short while men and women who had never given God a thought were intensely aware of God's reality. They trembled before his holiness. Their hearts melted as Jesus reached out to them in love and touched their lives in ways they would never be able to forget. But soon the blazing spiritual fire that tore through the towns and villages of Wales died away, leaving only a few glowing coals here and there.

The worldwide spiritual awakening that is now gathering momentum is different from past revivals in many respects. This revival is not localized. It is not limited to a particular language or nation. It is developing slowly, with roots in some places (like East Africa) that can be traced back a half century. From far-flung parts of the earth, reports keep reaching us of fresh outpourings of God's Spirit. Consider some highlights:

China

In 1950, when all missionaries were expelled, there were a total of four million Christians in China. Today many researchers put the number at one hundred million believers in Jesus, in a country where persecution has often been extreme. Most of this growth has taken place through house churches without the help of religious professionals and without the kind of financing that American churches consider essential.

Russia

One example of the spiritual awakening taking place in Russia is the work of Bruce Inglis of Chicago. In the summer months Bruce drives a moving van to support his family. In the winter months he visits Russia, where in six winters he and a handful of Russian co-workers have established one hundred congregations with over fifty Russian pastors.

Africa

Researchers put the number of Christians in Africa, as the twentieth century began, at ten million. By 1980 the number had multiplied to two hundred million. As we enter the twenty-first century that number will have doubled again to four hundred million followers of Jesus on a continent where war, famine and economic uncertainty have failed to dampen the fires of revival.

Latin America

There is hardly a country in Latin America that hasn't had some taste of revival during the last fifty years. Evangelical believers, whose numbers were placed at forty thousand to fifty thousand in 1900, have multiplied to well over one hundred million today.

Korea

Daily, at 5:00 A.M., tens of thousands of believers gather in their churches for prayer. One congregation, whose membership is approaching the million mark, reports twelve thousand new believers a month. In many Korean churches prayer and fasting are simply a normal part of the Christian life.

The Worldwide Messianic Movement

Messianic congregations and synagogues, made up of Jewish men and women who confess Yeshua as their Messiah, are multiplying, not only in North America, but in France, England, Australia, Israel, Turkey and Latin America. Are we looking at the beginning of the fulfillment of Paul's prophecy in Romans 11:24: "For if you have been cut from what is by nature a wild olive tree, and grafted, contrary to nature, into a cultivated olive tree, how much more will these natural branches be grafted back into their own olive tree"?

At the very least, this spreading global spiritual fire is a foretaste of what will one day be God's final worldwide wake-up call. The purpose of this revival, like every spiritual awakening before it, is to prepare the earth for its coming King: "Behold, I am coming soon, bringing my recompense, to repay every one for what he has done.... Blessed are those who wash their robes, that they may have the right to the tree of life" (Rv 22:12, 14).

You have been included in this plan. The fire of heaven descends into your heart, not for your sake alone, but for the sake of those whom the Spirit of the Lord intends to ignite through you. He sets fire to your heart so that you can be a torch in his hand.

If you are willing to be used by the Spirit on his terms and as he chooses, your life will become part of redemptive history. No one on earth may ever write a book about your exploits, but your life of obedience will make a difference—an eternal difference—in the lives God causes you to touch.

On the other hand, if you choose not to obey the call to obedience which the Lord Jesus has placed upon you through this revival, someone else will be raised up to accomplish the work that was meant to be yours. The work will be done, with you or without you. The word will go forth, through you or through someone else.

The opportunity is yours. If you accept this calling, your life will be linked to the life of a mighty army that is being raised to break through the gates of death and set the captives free before the King returns. All the power of heaven and earth will be placed at your disposal. And the Spirit of the King himself will accompany you every step of the way: "Lo, I am with you always, to the close of the age" (Mt 28:20).